EUGENE O'NEILL

Ah, Wilderness!

and

Days Without End

JONATHAN CAPE

THIRTY BEDFORD SQUARE LONDON

FIRST PUBLISHED IN GREAT BRITAIN 1934
REISSUED 1955
REPRINTED 1958
THIS PAPERBACK EDITION FIRST PUBLISHED 1973

JONATHAN CAPE LTD
30 BEDFORD SQUARE, LONDON WC1

ISBN 0 224 00878 1

Printed in Great Britain by
Fletcher & Son Ltd, Norwich
and bound by
Richard Clay (The Chaucer Press) Ltd, Bungay, Suffolk

Ah, Wilderness!

Scenes

ACT ONE

Sitting-room of the Miller home in a large small-town in Connecticut—early morning, July 4th, 1906.

ACT TWO

Dining-room of the Miller home—evening of the same day.

ACT THREE

Scene One : Back room of a bar in a small hotel—10 o'clock the same night.

Scene Two : Same as Act One—the sitting-room of the Miller home—a little after 11 o'clock the same night.

ACT FOUR

Scene One : The Miller sitting-room again—about 1 o'clock the following afternoon.

Scene Two : A strip of beach along the harbour—about 9 o'clock that night.

Scene Three : Same as Scene One—the sitting-room—about 10 o'clock the same night.

Characters

NAT MILLER, *owner of the " Evening Globe "*
ESSIE, *his wife*
ARTHUR ⎫
RICHARD ⎪ *their children*
MILDRED ⎬
TOMMY ⎭
SID DAVIS, *Essie's brother*
LILY MILLER, *Nat's sister*
DAVID McCOMBER
MURIEL McCOMBER, *his daughter*
WINT SELBY, *a classmate of Arthur's at Yale*
BELLE
NORAH
BARTENDER
SALESMAN

ACT ONE

SCENE. *Sitting-room of the Miller home in a large small-town in Connecticut—about* 7.30 *in the morning of July 4th,* 1906.

The room is fairly large, homely looking and cheerful in the morning sunlight, furnished with scrupulous medium-priced tastelessness of the period. Beneath the two windows at left, front, a sofa with silk and satin cushions stands against the wall. At rear of sofa, a bookcase with glass doors, filled with cheap sets, extends along the remaining length of wall. In the rear wall, left, is a double doorway with sliding doors and portières, leading into a dark, windowless, back parlour. At right of this doorway, another bookcase, this time a small, open one, crammed with boys' and girls' books and the best-selling novels of many past years—books the family really have read. To the right of this bookcase is the mate of the double doorway at its left, with sliding doors and portières, this one leading to a well-lighted front parlour. In the right wall, rear, a screen door opens on a porch. Farther forward in this wall are two windows, with a writing-desk and a chair between them. At centre is a big, round table with a green-shaded reading-lamp, the cord of the lamp running up to one of five sockets in the chandelier above. Five chairs are grouped about the table—three rockers at left, right, and right rear of it, two armchairs at rear and left rear. A medium-priced, inoffensive rug covers

11

most of the floor. The walls are papered white with a cheerful, ugly blue design.

Voices are heard in a conversational tone from the dining-room beyond the back parlour, where the family are just finishing breakfast. Then Mrs. Miller's voice, raised commandingly, "Tommy! Come back here and finish your milk!" At the same moment Tommy appears in the doorway from the back parlour—a chubby, sunburnt boy of eleven with dark eyes, blond hair wetted and plastered down in a parting, and a shiny, good-natured face, a rim of milk visible about his lips. Bursting with bottled-up energy and a longing to get started on the Fourth, he nevertheless has hesitated obediently at his mother's call.

TOMMY (*calls back pleadingly*). Aw, I'm full, Ma. And I said excuse me and you said all right. (*His Father's voice is heard speaking to his mother. Then she calls :* "All right, Tommy," *and Tommy asks eagerly.*) Can I go out now?

MOTHER'S VOICE (*correctingly*). May I !

TOMMY (*fidgeting, but obediently*). May I, Ma?

MOTHER'S VOICE. Yes. (*Tommy jumps for the screen door to the porch at right like a sprinter released by the starting-shot.*)

FATHER'S VOICE (*shouts after him*). But you set off your crackers away from the house, remember ! (*But Tommy is already through the screen door, which he leaves open behind him.*)

> (*A moment later the family appear from the back parlour, coming from the dining-room. First are Mildred and Arthur. Mildred is fifteen,*

tall and slender, with big, irregular features, resembling her father to the complete effacing of any pretence at prettiness. But her big, grey eyes are beautiful; she has vivacity and a fetching smile, and everyone thinks of her as an attractive girl. She is dressed in blouse and skirt in the fashion of the period.

Arthur, the eldest of the Miller children who are still living at home, is nineteen. He is tall, heavy, barrel-chested and muscular, the type of football linesman of that period, with a square, stolid face, small blue eyes and thick sandy hair. His manner is solemnly collegiate. He is dressed in the latest college fashion of that day, which has receded a bit from the extreme of preceding years, but still runs to padded shoulders and trousers half pegged at the top, and so small at their wide-cuffed bottoms that they cannot be taken off with shoes on.)

MILDRED (*as they appear—inquisitively*). Where are you going to-day, Art ?

ARTHUR (*with superior dignity*). That's my business. (*He ostentatiously takes from his pocket a tobacco pouch with a big " Υ " and class numerals stamped on it, and a heavy bulldog briar pipe with silver " Υ " and numerals, and starts filling the pipe.*)

MILDRED (*teasingly*). Bet I know, just the same ! Want me to tell you her initials ? E.R. ! (*She laughs.*)

(*Arthur, pleased by this insinuation at his lady-killing activities, yet finds it beneath his dignity to reply. He goes to the table, lights his pipe and picks up the local morning paper, and slouches back*

13

*into the armchair at left rear of table, beginning
to whistle " Oh, Waltz Me Around Again,
Willie" as he scans the headlines. Mildred
sits on the sofa at left, front.*

*Meanwhile, their mother and their Aunt
Lily, their father's sister, have appeared,
following them from the back parlour. Mrs.
Miller is around fifty, a short, stout woman
with fading light-brown hair sprinkled with
grey, who must have been decidedly pretty as
a girl in a round-faced, cute, small-featured,
wide-eyed fashion. She has big brown eyes,
soft and maternal—a bustling, mother-of-a-
family manner. She is dressed in blouse and
skirt.*

*Lily Miller, her sister-in-law, is forty-two,
tall, dark and thin. She conforms outwardly to
the conventional type of old-maid school teacher,
even to wearing glasses. But behind the
glasses her grey eyes are gentle and tired, and
her whole atmosphere is one of shy kindliness.
Her voice presents the greatest contrast to her
appearance—soft and full of sweetness. She,
also, is dressed in a blouse and skirt.)*

MRS. MILLER (*as they appear*). Getting milk down him
is like—— (*Suddenly she is aware of the screen door
standing half open.*) Goodness, look at that door he's
left open ! The house will be alive with flies ! (*Rush-
ing out to shut it.*) I've told him again and again—and
that's all the good it does ! It's just a waste of breath !
(*She slams the door shut.*)

LILY (*smiling*). Well, you can't expect a boy to remember to shut doors—on the Fourth of July. (*She goes*

diffidently to the straight-backed chair before the desk at right, front, leaving the comfortable chairs to the others.)

MRS. MILLER. That's you all over, Lily—always making excuses for him. You'll have him spoiled to death in spite of me. (*She sinks in rocker at right of table.*) Phew, I'm hot, aren't you ? This is going to be a scorcher. (*She picks up a magazine from the table and begins to rock, fanning herself.*)

> (*Meanwhile, her husband and her brother have appeared from the back parlour, both smoking cigars. Nat Miller is in his late fifties, a tall, dark, spare man, a little stoop-shouldered, more than a little bald, dressed with an awkward attempt at sober respectability imposed upon an innate heedlessness of clothes. His long face has large, irregular, undistinguished features, but he has fine, shrewd, humorous grey eyes.*
>
> *Sid Davis, his brother-in-law, is forty-five, short and fat, bald-headed, with the Puckish face of a Peck's Bad Boy who has never grown up. He is dressed in what had once been a very natty loud light suit but is now a shapeless and faded nondescript in cut and colour.*)

SID (*as they appear*). Oh, I like the job first rate, Nat. Waterbury's a nifty old town with the lid off, when you get to know the ropes. I rang in a joke in one of my stories that tickled the folks there pink. Waterwagon —Waterbury—Waterloo !

MILLER (*grinning*). Darn good !

SID (*pleased*). I thought it was pretty fair myself. (*Goes on a bit ruefully, as if oppressed by a secret sorrow.*)

Yes, you can see life in Waterbury, all right——that is, if you're looking for life in Waterbury !

MRS. MILLER.   What's that about Waterbury, Sid ?

SID.   I was saying it's all right in its way——but there's no place like home.

> (*As if to punctuate this remark, there begins a series of bangs from just beyond the porch outside, as Tommy inaugurates his celebration by setting off a package of firecrackers. The assembled family jump in their chairs.*)

MRS. MILLER.   That boy ! (*She rushes to the screen door and out on the porch, calling :*) Tommy ! You mind what your Pa told you ! You take your crackers out in the back-yard, you hear me !

ARTHUR (*frowning scornfully*).   Fresh kid ! He did it on purpose to scare us.

MILLER (*grinning through his annoyance*).   Darned youngster ! He'll have the house afire before the day's out.

SID (*grins and sings*).

> " Dunno what ter call 'im
> But he's mighty like a Rose——velt."

> (*They all laugh.*)

LILY.   Sid, you Crazy !

> (*Sid beams at her. Mrs. Miller comes back from the porch, still fuming.*)

MRS. MILLER.   Well, I've made him go out back at last. Now we'll have a little peace.

(*As if to contradict this, the bang of firecrackers and torpedoes begins from the rear of the house, left, and continues at intervals throughout the scene, not nearly so loud as the first explosion, but sufficiently emphatic to form a disturbing punctuation to the conversation.*)

MILLER. Well, what's on the tappee for all of you to-day ? Sid, you're coming to the Sachem Club picnic with me, of course.

SID (*a bit embarrassedly*). You bet. I mean I'd like to, Nat—that is, if——

MRS. MILLER (*regarding her brother with smiling suspicion*). Hmm ! I know what that Sachem Club picnics always meant !

LILY (*breaks in in a forced joking tone that conceals a deep earnestness*). No, not this time, Essie. Sid's a reformed character since he's been on the paper in Waterbury. At least, that's what he swore to me last night.

SID (*avoiding her eyes, humiliated—joking it off*). Pure as the driven snow, that's me. They're running me for president of the W.C.T.U.

(*They all laugh.*)

MRS. MILLER. Sid, you're a caution. You turn everything into a joke. But you be careful, you hear ? We're going to have dinner in the evening to-night, you know —the best shore dinner you ever tasted and I don't want you coming home—well, not able to appreciate it.

LILY. Oh, I know he'll be careful to-day. Won't you, Sid ?

SID (*more embarrassed than ever—joking it off melo-*

dramatically). Lily, I swear to you if any man offers me a drink, I'll kill him—that is, if he changes his mind !

(*They all laugh except Lily, who bites her lip and stiffens.*)

MRS. MILLER. No use talking to him, Lily. You ought to know better by this time. We can only hope for the best.

MILLER. Now, you women stop picking on Sid. It's the Fourth of July and even a downtrodden newspaper-man has a right to enjoy himself when he's on his holiday.

MRS. MILLER. I wasn't thinking only of Sid.

MILLER (*with a wink at the others*). What, are you insinuating I ever—— ?

MRS. MILLER. Well, to do you justice, no, not what you'd really call—— But I've known you to come back from this darned Sachem Club picnic—— Well, I didn't need any little bird to whisper that you'd been some place besides to the well ! (*She smiles good-naturedly. Miller chuckles.*)

SID (*after a furtive glance at the stiff and silent Lily—changes the subject abruptly by turning to Arthur*). How are you spending the festive Fourth, Boola-Boola ?

(*Arthur stiffens dignifiedly.*)

MILDRED (*teasingly*). I can tell you, if he won't.

MRS. MILLER (*smiling*). Off to the Rands', I suppose.

ARTHUR (*with dignity*). I and Bert Turner are taking Elsie and Ethel Rand canoeing. We're going to have a picnic lunch on Strawberry Island. And this evening I'm staying at the Rands' for dinner.

MILLER. You're accounted for, then. How about you, Mid ?

MILDRED. I'm going to the beach to Anne Culver's.

ARTHUR (*sarcastically*). Of course, there won't be any boys present ! Johnny Dodd, for example ?

MILDRED (*giggles—then with a coquettish toss of her head*). Pooh ! What do I care for him ? He's not the only pebble on the beach.

MILLER. Stop your everlasting teasing, you two. How about you and Lily, Essie ?

MRS. MILLER. I don't know. I haven't made any plans. Have you, Lily ?

LILY (*quietly*). No. Anything you want to do.

MRS. MILLER. Well, I thought we'd just sit around and rest and talk.

MILLER. You can gossip any day. This is the Fourth. Now, I've got a better suggestion than that. What do you say to an automobile ride ? I'll get out the Buick and we'll drive around town and out to the lighthouse and back. Then Sid and I will let you off here, or anywhere you say, and we'll go on to the picnic.

MRS. MILLER. I'd love it. Wouldn't you, Lily ?

LILY. It would be nice.

MILLER. Then, that's all settled.

SID (*embarrassedly*). Lily, want to come with me to the fireworks display at the beach to-night ?

MRS. MILLER. That's right, Sid. You take her out.

Poor Lily never has any fun, always sitting home with me.

LILY (*flustered and grateful*). I—I'd like to, Sid, thank you. (*Then an apprehensive look comes over her face.*) Only not if you come home—you know.

SID (*again embarrassed and humiliated—again joking it off, solemnly*). Evil-minded, I'm afraid, Nat. I hate to say it of your sister.

> (*They all laugh. Even Lily cannot suppress a smile.*)

ARTHUR (*with heavy jocularity*). Listen, Uncle Sid. Don't let me catch you and Aunt Lily spooning on a bench to-night—or it'll be my duty to call a cop !

> (*Sid and Lily both look painfully embarrassed at this, and the joke falls flat, except for Mildred who can't restrain a giggle at the thought of these two ancients spooning.*)

MRS. MILLER (*rebukingly*). Arthur !

MILLER (*dryly*). That'll do you. Your education in kicking a football around Yale seems to have blunted your sense of humour.

MRS. MILLER (*suddenly—startledly*). But where's Richard ? We're forgetting all about him. Why, where is that boy ? I thought he came in with us from breakfast.

MILDRED. I'll bet he's off somewhere writing a poem to Muriel McComber, the silly ! Or pretending to write one. I think he just copies——

ARTHUR (*looking back toward the dining-room*). He's still in the dining-room, reading a book. (*Turning back*

—*scornfully*.) Gosh, he's always reading now. It's not my idea of having a good time in vacation.

MILLER (*caustically*). He read his school books, too, strange as that may seem to you. That's why he came out top of his class. I'm hoping before you leave New Haven they'll find time to teach you reading is a good habit.

MRS. MILLER (*sharply*). That reminds me, Nat. I've been meaning to speak to you about those awful books Richard is reading. You've got to give him a good talking to—— (*She gets up from her chair.*) I'll go up and get them right now. I found them where he'd hid them on the shelf in his wardrobe. You just wait till you see what——

(*She bustles off, rear right, through the front parlour.*)

MILLER (*plainly not relishing whatever is coming—to Sid, grumblingly*). Seems to me she might wait until the Fourth is over before bringing up—— (*Then with a grin.*) I know there's nothing to it, anyway. When I think of the books I used to sneak off and read when I was a kid.

SID. Me, too. I suppose Dick is deep in Nick Carter or Old Cap Collier.

MILLER. No, he passed that period long ago. Poetry's his red meat nowadays, I think—love poetry —and socialism, too, I suspect, from some dire declarations he's made. (*Then briskly.*) Well, might as well get him on the carpet. (*He calls.*) Richard. (*No answer—louder.*) Richard. (*No answer—then in a bellow.*) Richard !

ARTHUR (*shouting*). Hey, Dick, wake up ! Pa's calling you.

RICHARD's VOICE (*from the dining-room*). All right. I'm coming.

MILLER. Darn him ! When he gets his nose in a book, the house could fall down and he'd never——

> (*Richard appears in the doorway from the back par-lour, the book he has been reading in one hand, a finger marking his place. He looks a bit startled still, reluctantly called back to earth from another world.*
>
> *He is going on seventeen, just out of high school. In appearance he is a perfect blend of father and mother, so much so that each is con-vinced he is the image of the other. He has his mother's light-brown hair, his father's grey eyes ; his features are neither large nor small ; he is of medium height, neither fat nor thin. One would not call him a handsome boy ; neither is he homely. But he is definitely different from both of his parents, too. There is something of extreme sensitiveness added— a restless, apprehensive, defiant, shy, dreamy self-conscious intelligence about him. In man-ner he is alternately plain simple boy and a posy actor solemnly playing a rôle. He is dressed in prep. school reflection of the college style of Arthur.*)

RICHARD. Did you want me, Pa ?

MILLER. I'd hoped I'd made that plain. Come and sit down a while. (*He points to the rocking chair at the right of table near his.*)

RICHARD (*coming forward—seizing on the opportunity to*

play up his preoccupation—with apologetic superiority).   I didn't hear you, Pa.   I was off in another world.

> (*Mildred slyly shoves her foot out so that he trips over it, almost falling.   She laughs gleefully.   So does Arthur.*)

ARTHUR.   Good for you, Mid !   That'll wake him up !

RICHARD (*grins sheepishly—all boy now*).   Darn you, Mid !   I'll show you !

> (*He pushes her back on the sofa and tickles her with his free hand, still holding the book in the other.   She shrieks.*)

ARTHUR.   Give it to her, Dick !

MILLER.   That's enough, now.   No more rough-house.   You sit down here, Richard.

> (*Richard obediently takes the chair at right of table, opposite his father.*)

What were you planning to do with yourself to-day ? Going out to the beach with Mildred ?

RICHARD (*scornfully superior*).   That silly skirt party ! I should say not !

MILDRED.   He's not coming because Muriel isn't. I'll bet he's got a date with her somewheres.

RICHARD (*flushing bashfully*).   You shut up !   (*Then to his father.*)   I thought I'd just stay home, Pa—this morning, anyway.

MILLER.   Help Tommy set off firecrackers, eh ?

RICHARD (*drawing himself up—with dignity*).   I should

say not. (*Then frowning portentously.*) I don't believe in this silly celebrating the Fourth of July—all this lying talk about liberty—when there is no liberty !

MILLER (*a twinkle in his eye*). Hmm.

RICHARD (*getting warmed up*). The land of the free and the home of the brave ! Home of the slave is what they ought to call it—the wage slave ground under the heel of the capitalist class, starving, crying for bread for his children, and all he gets is a stone ! The Fourth of July is a stupid farce !

MILLER (*putting a hand to his mouth to conceal a grin*). Hmm. Them are mighty strong words. You'd better not repeat such sentiments outside the bosom of the family or they'll have you in jail.

SID. And throw away the key.

RICHARD (*darkly*). Let them put me in jail. But how about the freedom of speech in the Constitution, then ? That must be a farce, too. (*Then he adds grimly.*) No, you can celebrate your Fourth of July. I'll celebrate the day the people bring out the guillotine again and I see Pierpont Morgan being driven by in a tumbril !

> (*His father and Sid are greatly amused ; Lily is shocked but taking her cue from them, smiles. Mildred stares at him in puzzled wonderment, never having heard this particular line before. Only Arthur betrays the outraged reaction of a patriot.*)

ARTHUR. Aw say, you fresh kid, tie that bull outside ! You ought to get a punch in the nose for talking that way on the Fourth !

MILLER (*solemnly*). Son, if I didn't know it was you talking, I'd think we had Emma Goldman with us.

ARTHUR. Never mind, Pa. Wait till we get him down to Yale. We'll take that out of him !

RICHARD (*with high scorn*). Oh, Yale ! You think there's nothing in the world besides Yale. After all, what is Yale ?

ARTHUR. You'll find out what !

SID (*provocatively*). Don't let them scare you, Dick. Give 'em hell !

LILY (*shocked*). Sid ! You shouldn't swear be-fore——

RICHARD. What do you think I am, Aunt Lily—a baby ? I've heard worse than anything Uncle Sid says.

MILDRED. And said worse himself, I bet.

MILLER (*with a comic air of resignation*). Well, Richard, I've always found I've had to listen to at least one stump speech every Fourth. I only hope getting your extra strong one right after breakfast will let me off for the rest of the day. (*They all laugh now, taking this as a cue.*)

RICHARD (*sombrely*). That's right, laugh ! After you, the deluge, you think ! But look out ! Supposing it comes before ? Why shouldn't the workers of the world unite and rise ? They have nothing to lose but their chains ! (*He recites threateningly.*) " The days grow hot, O Babylon ! 'Tis cool beneath thy willow trees ! "

MILLER. Hmm. That's good. But where's the connection, exactly ? Something from that book you're reading ?

RICHARD (*superior*). No. That's poetry. This is prose.

MILLER. I've heard there was a difference between 'em. What is the book ?

RICHARD (*importantly*). Carlyle's " French Revolution."

MILLER. Hmm. So that's where you drove the tumbril from and piled poor old Pierpont in it. (*Then seriously.*) Glad you're reading it, Richard. It's a darn fine book.

RICHARD (*with unflattering astonishment*). What, have you read it ?

MILLER. Well, you see, even a newspaper owner can't get out of reading a book every now and again.

RICHARD (*abashed*). I—I didn't mean—I know you —— (*Then enthusiastically.*) Say, isn't it a great book, though—that part about Mirabeau—and about Marat and Robespierre——

MRS. MILLER (*appears from the front parlour in a great state of flushed annoyance*). Never you mind Robespierre, young man ! You tell me this minute where you've hidden those books ! They were on the shelf in your wardrobe and now you've gone and hid them somewheres else. You go right up and bring them to your father !

(*Richard, for a second, looks suddenly guilty and crushed. Then he bristles defensively.*)

MILLER (*after a quick understanding glance at him*). Never mind his getting them now. We'll waste the whole morning over those darned books. And anyway,

26

he has a right to keep his library to himself—that is, if they're not too—— What books are they, Richard ?

RICHARD (*self-consciously*). Well—there's——

MRS. MILLER. I'll tell you, if he won't—and you give him a good talking to. (*Then, after a glance at Richard, mollifiedly.*) Not that I blame Richard. There must be some boy he knows who's trying to show off as advanced and wicked, and he told him about——

RICHARD. No ! I read about them myself, in the papers and in other books.

MRS. MILLER. Well, no matter how, there they were on his shelf. Two by that awful Oscar Wilde they put in jail for heaven knows what wickedness.

ARTHUR (*suddenly—solemnly authoritative*). He committed bigamy. (*Then as Sid smothers a burst of ribald laughter.*) What are you laughing at ? I guess I ought to know. A fellow at college told me. His father was in England when this Wilde was pinched—and he said he remembered once his mother asked his father about it and he told her he'd committed bigamy.

MILLER (*hiding a smile behind his hand*). Well then, that must be right, Arthur.

MRS. MILLER. I wouldn't put it past him, nor anything else. One book was called the Picture of something or other.

RICHARD. " The Picture of Dorian Gray." It's one of the greatest novels ever written !

MRS. MILLER. Looked to me like cheap trash. And the second book was poetry. The Ballad of I forget what.

RICHARD. " The Ballad of Reading Gaol," one of the greatest poems ever written. (*He pronounces it Reading Goal [as in goalpost].*)

MRS. MILLER. All about someone who murdered his wife and got hung, as he richly deserved, as far as I could make out. And then there were two books by that Bernard Shaw——

RICHARD. The greatest playwright alive to-day !

MRS. MILLER. To hear him tell it, maybe ! You know, Nat, the one who wrote a play about—well, never mind—that was so vile they wouldn't even let it play in New York !

MILLER. Hmm. I remember.

MRS. MILLER. One was a book of his plays and the other had a long title I couldn't make head or tail of, only it wasn't a play.

RICHARD (*proudly*). " The Quintessence of Ibsenism."

MILDRED. Phew ! Good gracious, what a name ! What does it mean, Dick ? I'll bet he doesn't know.

RICHARD (*outraged*). I do, too, know ! It's about Ibsen, the greatest playwright since Shakespeare !

MRS. MILLER. Yes, there was a book of plays by that Ibsen there, too ! And poems by Swin something——

RICHARD. " Poems and Ballads by Swinburne," Ma. The greatest poet since Shelley ! He tells the truth about real love !

MRS. MILLER. Love ! Well, all I can´say is, from reading here and there, that if he wasn't flung in jail

along with Wilde, he should have been. Some of the things I simply couldn't read, they were so indecent——
All about—well, I can't tell you before Lily and Mildred.

SID (*with a wink at Richard—jokingly*). Remember, I'm next on that one, Dick. I feel the need of a little poetical education.

LILY (*scandalized, but laughing*). Sid ! Aren't you ashamed ?

MRS. MILLER. This is no laughing matter. And then there was Kipling—but I suppose he's not so bad. And last there was a poem—a long one—the Rubay——
What is it, Richard ?

RICHARD. "The Rubaiyat of Omar Khayyám." That's the best of all !

MILLER. Oh, I've read that, Essie—got a copy down at the office.

SID (*enthusiastically*). So have I. It's a pippin !

LILY (*with shy excitement*). I—I've read it, too—at the library. I like—some parts of it.

MRS. MILLER (*scandalized*). Why, Lily !

MILLER. Everybody's reading that now, Essie—and it don't seem to do them any harm. There's fine things in it, seems to me—true things.

MRS. MILLER (*a bit bewildered and uncertain now*). Why, Nat, I don't see how you—— It looked terrible blasphemous—parts I read.

SID. Remember this one : (*he quotes rhetorically*) "Oh Thou, who didst with pitfall and gin beset the path I was to wander in———" Now, I've always noticed how beset my path was with gin—in the past, you understand !

> (*He casts a joking side glance at Lily. The others laugh. But Lily is in a melancholy dream and hasn't heard him.*)

MRS. MILLER (*tartly, but evidently suppressing her usual smile where he is concerned*). You would pick out the ones with liquor in them !

LILY (*suddenly—with a sad pathos, quotes awkwardly and shyly*). I like—because it's true :

" The Moving Finger writes, and having writ,
    Moves on : nor all your Piety nor Wit
    Shall lure it back to cancel half a Line,
    Nor all your Tears wash out a Word of it."

MRS. MILLER (*astonished, as are all the others*). Why, Lily, I never knew you to recite poetry before !

LILY (*immediately guilty and apologetic*). I—it just stuck in my memory somehow.

RICHARD (*looking at her as if he had never seen her before*). Good for you, Aunt Lily ! (*Then enthusiastically.*) But that isn't the best. The best is :

" A Book of Verses underneath the Bough,
    A Jug of Wine, A Loaf of Bread—and Thou
    Beside me singing in the Wilderness———"

ARTHUR (*who, bored to death by all this poetry quoting, has wandered over to the window at rear of desk, right*). Hey ! Look who's coming up the walk——— Old Man McComber !

MILLER (*irritably*). Dave ? . Now what in thunder does that damned old——— Sid, I can see where we never are going to get to that picnic.

MRS. MILLER (*vexatiously*). He'll know we're in this early, too. No use lying. (*Then appalled by another thought.*) That Norah——she's that thick, she never can answer the front door right unless I tell her each time. Nat, you've got to talk to Dave. I'll have her show him in here. Lily, you run up the back stairs and get your things on. I'll be up in a second. Nat, you get rid of him the first second you can ! Whatever can the old fool want———

(*She and Lily hurry out through the back parlour.*)

ARTHUR. I'm going to beat it—just time to catch the eight-twenty trolley.

MILDRED. I've got to catch that, too. Wait till I get my hat, Art !

(*She rushes into the back parlour.*)

ARTHUR (*shouts after her*). I can't wait. You can catch up with me if you hurry. (*He turns at the back-parlour door—with a grin.*) McComber may be coming to see if your intentions toward his daughter are dishonourable, Dick ! You'd better beat it while your shoes are good !

(*He disappears through the back-parlour door, laughing.*)

RICHARD (*a bit shaken, but putting on a brave front*). Think I'm scared of him ?

MILLER (*gazing at him—frowning*). Can't imagine what——— But it's to complain about something, I

31

know that. I only wish I didn't have to be pleasant with the old buzzard—but he's about the most valuable advertiser I've got.

SID (*sympathetically*). I know. But tell him to go to hell, anyway. He needs that ad more than you.

> (*The sound of the bell comes from the rear of the house, off left from back parlour.*)

MILLER. There he is. You clear out, Dick—but come right back as soon as he's gone, you hear ? I'm not through with you, yet.

RICHARD. Yes, Pa.

MILLER. You better clear out, too, Sid. You know Dave doesn't approve jokes.

SID. And loves me like poison ! Come on, Dick, we'll go out and help Tommy celebrate.

> (*He takes Richard's arm and they also disappear through the back-parlour door. Miller glances through the front parlour toward the front door, then calls in a tone of strained heartiness.*)

MILLER. Hello, Dave. Come right in here. What good wind blows you around on this glorious Fourth ?

> (*A flat, brittle voice answers him : " Good morning," and a moment later David McComber appears in the doorway from the front parlour. He is a thin, dried-up little man with a head too large for his body perched on a scrawny neck, and a long solemn horse face with deep-set little black eyes, a blunt formless nose and a tiny slit of a mouth. He is about the same age as Miller but is entirely bald, and looks*)

*ten years older. He is dressed with a prim
neatness in shiny old black clothes.)*

Here, sit down and make yourself comfortable. (*Holding
out the cigar-box.*) Have a cigar ?

MCCOMBER (*sitting down in the chair at the right of table
—acidly*). You're forgetting. I never smoke.

MILLER (*forcing a laugh at himself*). That's so. So I
was. Well, I'll smoke alone then. (*He bites off the end
of the cigar viciously, as if he wished it were McComber's
head, and sits down opposite him.*)

MCCOMBER. You asked me what brings me here, so
I'll come to the point at once. I regret to say it's something disagreeable—disgraceful would be nearer the
truth—and it concerns your son, Richard !

MILLER (*beginning to bristle—but calmly*). Oh, come
now, Dave, I'm sure Richard hasn't——

MCCOMBER (*sharply*). And I'm positive he has.
You're not accusing me of being a liar, I hope.

MILLER. No one said anything about liar. I only
meant you're surely mistaken if you think——

MCCOMBER. I'm not mistaken. I have proof of
everything in his own handwriting !

MILLER (*sharply*). Let's get down to brass tacks. Just
what is it you're charging him with ?

MCCOMBER. With being dissolute and blasphemous
—with deliberately attempting to corrupt the morals of
my young daughter Muriel.

MILLER. Then I'm afraid I will have to call you a liar,
Dave !

MCCOMBER (*without taking offence—in the same flat, brittle voice*). I thought you'd get around to that, so I brought some of the proofs with me. I've a lot more of 'em at home. (*He takes a wallet from his inside coat pocket, selects five or six slips of paper, and holds them out to Miller.*) These are good samples of the rest. My wife discovered them in one of Muriel's bureau drawers hidden under the underwear. They're all in his handwriting, you can't deny it. Anyway, Muriel's confessed to me he wrote them. You read them and then say I'm a liar.

(*Miller has taken the slips and is reading them frowningly. McComber talks on.*)

Evidently you've been too busy to take the right care about Richard's bringing up or what he's allowed to read—though I can't see why his mother failed in her duty. But that's your misfortune, and none of my business. But Muriel is my business and I can't and I won't have her innocence exposed to the contamination of a young man whose mind, judging from his choice of reading matter, is as foul——

MILLER (*making a tremendous effort to control his temper*). Why, you damned old fool ! Can't you see Richard's only a fool kid who's just at the stage when he's out to rebel against all authority, and so he grabs at everything radical to read and wants to pass it on to his elders and his girl and boy friends to show off what a young hellion he is ! Why, at heart you'd find Richard is just as innocent and as big a kid as Muriel is ! (*He pushes the slips of paper across the table contemptuously.*) This stuff doesn't mean anything to me—that is, nothing of what you think it means. If you believe this would corrupt Muriel, then you must believe she's easily corrupted ! But I'll bet you'd find she knows a lot more about life than you give

34

her credit for—and can guess a stork didn't bring her down your chimney !

MCCOMBER. Now you're insulting my daughter. I won't forget that.

MILLER. I'm not insulting her. I think Muriel is a darn nice girl. That's why I'm giving her credit for ordinary good sense. I'd say the same about my own Mildred, who's the same age.

MCCOMBER. I know nothing about your Mildred except that she's known all over as a flirt. (*Then more sharply.*) Well, I knew you'd prove obstinate, but I certainly never dreamed you'd have the impudence, after reading those papers, to claim your son was innocent of all wrongdoing !

MILLER. And what did you dream I'd do ?

MCCOMBER. Do what it's your plain duty to do as a citizen to protect other people's children ! Take and give him a hiding he'd remember to the last day of his life ! You'd ought to do it for his sake, if you had any sense—unless you want him to end up in jail !

MILLER (*his fists clenched, leans across the table*). Dave, I've stood all I can stand from you ! You get out ! And get out quick, if you don't want a kick in the rear to help you !

MCCOMBER (*again in his flat, brittle voice, slowly getting to his feet*). You needn't lose your temper. I'm only demanding you do your duty by your own as I've already done by mine. I'm punishing Muriel. She's not to be allowed out of the house for a month and she's to be in bed every night by eight sharp. And yet she's blameless, compared to that——

35

MILLER. I said I'd had enough out of you, Dave ! (*He makes a threatening movement.*)

MCCOMBER. You needn't lay hands on me. I'm going. But there's one thing more. (*He takes a letter from his wallet.*) Here's a letter from Muriel for your son. (*Puts it on the table.*) It makes clear, I think, how she's come to think about him, now that her eyes have been opened. I hope he heeds what's inside— for his own good and yours—because if I ever catch him hanging about my place again I'll have him arrested ! And don't think I'm not going to make you regret the insults you've heaped on me. I'm taking the advertisement for my store out of your paper—and it won't go in again, I tell you, not unless you apologize in writing and promise to punish——

MILLER. I'll see you in hell first ! As for your damned old ad, take it out and go to hell !

MCCOMBER. That's plain bluff. You know how badly you need it. So do I. (*He starts stiffly for the door.*)

MILLER. Here ! Listen a minute ! I'm just going to call *your* bluff and tell you that, whether you want to reconsider your decision or not, I'm going to refuse to print your damned ad after to-morrow ! Put that in your pipe and smoke it ! Furthermore, I'll start a campaign to encourage outside capital to open a dry-goods store in opposition to you that won't be the public swindle I can prove yours is !

MCCOMBER (*a bit shaken by this threat—but in the same flat tone*). I'll sue you for libel.

MILLER. When I get through, there won't be a person in town will buy a dish-rag in your place !

MCCOMBER (*more shaken, his eyes shifting about furtively*). That's all bluff. You wouldn't dare—— (*Then finally he says uncertainly :*) Well, good day. (*And turns and goes out.*)

> (*Nat stands looking after him. Slowly the anger drains from his face and leaves him looking a bit sick and disgusted. Sid appears from the back parlour. He is nursing a burn on his right hand, but his face is one broad grin of satisfaction.*)

SID. I burned my hand with one of Tommy's damned firecrackers and came in to get some vaseline. I was listening to the last of your scrap. Good for you, Nat ! You sure gave him hell !

MILLER (*dully*). Much good it'll do. He knows it was all talk.

SID. That's just what he don't know, Nat. The old skinflint has a guilty conscience.

MILLER. Well, anyone who knows me knows I wouldn't use my paper for a dirty, spiteful trick like that—no matter what he did to me.

SID. Yes, everyone knows you're an old sucker, Nat, too decent for your own good. But McComber never saw you like this before. I tell you you scared the pants off him. (*He chuckles.*)

MILLER (*still dejectedly*). I don't know what made me let go like that. The hell of skunks like McComber is that after being with them ten minutes you become as big skunks as they are.

SID (*notices the slips of paper on the table*). What's this ?

Something he brought ? (*He picks them up and starts to read.*)

MILLER (*grimly*). Samples of the new freedom—from those books Essie found—that Richard's been passing on to Muriel to educate her. They're what started the rumpus. (*Then frowning.*) I've got to do something about that young anarchist or he'll be getting me, and himself, in a peck of trouble. (*Then pathetically helpless.*) But what can I do ? Putting the curb bit on would make him worse. Then he'd have a harsh tyrant to defy. He'd love that, darn him !

SID (*has been reading the slips, a broad grin on his face —suddenly he whistles*). Phew ! This is a warm lulu for fair ! (*He recites with a joking intensity.*)

" My life is bitter with thy love ; thine eyes
    Blind me, thy tresses burn me, thy sharp sighs
    Divide my flesh and spirit with soft sound——"

MILLER (*with a grim smile*). Hmm. I missed that one. That must be Mr. Swinburne's copy. I've never read him, but I've heard something like that was the matter with him.

SID. Yes, it's labelled Swinburne—" Anactoria." Whatever that is. But wait, watch and listen ! The worst is yet to come ! (*He recites with added comic intensity :*)

" That I could drink thy veins as wine, and eat
    Thy breasts like honey, that from face to feet
    Thy body were abolished and consumed,
    And in my flesh thy very flesh entombed ! "

MILLER (*an irrepressible boyish grin coming to his face*).

Hell and hallelujah ! Just picture old Dave digesting that for the first time ! Gosh, I'd give a lot to have seen his face ! (*Then a trace of shocked reproof showing in his voice.*) But it's no joking matter. That stuff *is* warm —too damned warm, if you ask me ! I don't like this a damned bit, Sid. That's no kind of thing to be sending a decent girl. (*More worriedly.*) I thought he was really stuck on her—as one gets stuck on a decent girl at his age—all moonshine and holding hands and a kiss now and again. But this looks—I wonder if he is hanging around her to see what he can get ? (*Angrily.*) By God, if that's true, he deserves that licking McComber says it's my duty to give him ! I've got to draw the line somewhere !

SID. Yes, it won't do to have him getting any decent girl in trouble.

MILLER. The only thing I can do is put it up to him straight. (*With pride.*) Richard'll stand up to his guns, no matter what. I've never known him to lie to me.

SID (*at a noise from the back parlour, looks that way—in a whisper*). Then now's your chance. I'll beat it and leave you alone—see if the women folks are ready upstairs. We ought to get started soon—if we're ever going to make that picnic.

> (*He is half-way to the entrance to the front parlour as Richard enters from the back parlour, very evidently nervous about McComber's call.*)

RICHARD (*adopting a forced, innocent tone*). How's your hand, Uncle Sid ?

SID. All right, Dick, thanks—only hurts a little.

(He disappears. Miller watches his son frowningly. Richard gives him a quick side glance and grows more guiltily self-conscious.)

RICHARD *(forcing a snicker)*. Gee, Pa, Uncle Sid's a bigger kid than Tommy is. He was throwing fire-crackers in the air and catching them on the back of his hand and throwing 'em off again just before they went off—and one came and he wasn't quick enough, and it went off almost on top of——

MILLER. Never mind that. I've got something else to talk to you about besides firecrackers.

RICHARD *(apprehensively)*. What, Pa?

MILLER *(suddenly puts both hands on his shoulders—quietly)*. Look here, Son. I'm going to ask you a question, and I want an honest answer. I warn you before-hand if the answer is " yes " I'm going to punish you and punish you hard because you'll have done something no boy of mine ought to do. But you've never lied to me before, I know, and I don't believe, even to save yourself punishment, you'd lie to me now, would you?

RICHARD *(impressed—with dignity)*. I won't lie, Pa.

MILLER. Have you been trying to have something to do with Muriel—something you shouldn't—you know what I mean.

RICHARD *(stares at him for a moment, as if he couldn't com-prehend—then, as he does, a look of shocked indignation comes over his face)*. No ! What do you think I am, Pa ? I never would ! She's not that kind ! Why, I—I love her ! I'm going to marry her—after I get out of college ! She's said she would ! We're engaged !

40

MILLER (*with great relief*). All right. That's all I wanted to know. We won't talk any more about it. (*He gives him an approving pat on the back.*)

RICHARD. I don't see how you could think—— Did that old idiot McComber say that about me ?

MILLER (*joking now*). Shouldn't call your future father-in-law names, should you ? 'Tain't respectful. (*Then after a glance at Richard's indignant face—points to the slips of paper on the table.*) Well, you can't exactly blame old Dave, can you, when you read through that literature you wished on his innocent daughter ?

RICHARD (*sees the slips for the first time and is overcome by embarrassment, which he immediately tries to cover up with a superior carelessness*). Oh, so that's why. He found those, did he ? I told her to be careful—— Well, it'll do him good to read the truth about life for once and get rid of his old-fogy ideas.

MILLER. I'm afraid I've got to agree with him, though, that they're hardly fit reading for a young girl. (*Then with subtle flattery.*) They're all well enough, in their way, for you who're a man, but—— Think it over, and see if you don't agree with me.

RICHARD (*embarrassedly*). Aw, I only did it because I liked them—and I wanted her to face life as it is. She's so darned afraid of life—afraid of her Old Man—afraid of people saying this or that about her—afraid of being in love—afraid of everything. She's even afraid to let me kiss her. I thought, maybe, reading those things— they're beautiful, aren't they, Pa ?—I thought they would give her the spunk to lead her own life, and not be— always thinking of being afraid.

MILLER. I see. Well, I'm afraid she's still afraid. (*He takes the letter from the table.*) Here's a letter from her he said to give you.

> (*Richard takes the letter from him uncertainly, his expression changing to one of apprehension.*)

(*Miller adds with a kindly smile :*) You better be prepared for a bit of a blow. But never mind. There's lots of other fish in the sea.

> (*Richard is not listening to him, but staring at the letter with a sort of fascinated dread. Miller looks into his son's face a second, then turns away, troubled and embarrassed.*)

Darn it ! I better go upstairs and get rigged out or I never will get to that picnic.

> (*He moves awkwardly and self-consciously off through the front parlour. Richard continues to stare at the letter for a moment—then girds up his courage and tears it open and begins to read swiftly. As he reads, his face grows more and more wounded and tragic, until at the end his mouth draws down at the corners, as if he were about to break into tears. With an effort he forces them back and his face grows flushed with humiliation and wronged anger.*)

RICHARD (*blurts out to himself*). The little coward ! I hate her ! She can't treat me like that ! I'll show her !

> (*At the sound of voices from the front parlour, he quickly shoves the letter into the inside pocket of his coat and does his best to appear calm and indifferent, even attempting to whistle " Waiting at the Church." But the whistle*

peters out miserably as his mother, Lily and Sid enter from the front parlour. They are dressed in all the elaborate paraphernalia of motoring at that period—linen dusters, veils, goggles, Sid in a snappy cap.)

MRS. MILLER. Well, we're about ready to start at last, thank goodness ! Let's hope no more callers are on the way. What did that McComber want, Richard, do you know ? Sid couldn't tell us.

RICHARD. You can search me. Ask Pa.

MRS. MILLER *(immediately sensing something " down " in his manner—going to him worriedly).* Why, whatever's the matter with you, Richard ? You sound as if you'd lost your last friend ! What is it ?

RICHARD *(desperately).* I—I don't feel so well—my stomach's sick.

MRS. MILLER *(immediately all sympathy—smoothing his hair back from his forehead).* You poor boy ! What a shame—on the Fourth, too, of all days ! *(Turning to the others.)* Maybe I better stay home with him, if he's sick.

LILY. Yes, I'll stay, too.

RICHARD *(more desperately).* No ! You go, Ma ! I'm not really sick. I'll be all right. You go. I want to be alone ! *(Then, as a louder bang comes from in back as Tommy sets off a cannon cracker, he jumps to his feet.)* Darn Tommy and his darned firecrackers ! You can't get any peace in this house with that darned kid around ! Darn the Fourth of July, anyway ! I wish we still belonged to England ! *(He strides off in an indignant fury of misery through the front parlour.)*

MRS. MILLER (*stares after him worriedly—then sighs philosophically*).   Well, I guess he can't be so very sick—after that.   (*She shakes her head.*)   He's a queer boy.   Sometimes I can't make head or tail of him.

MILLER (*calls from the front door beyond the back parlour*). Come along, folks.   Let's get started.

SID.   We're coming, Nat.

> (*He and the two women move off through the front parlour.*)

CURTAIN

ACT TWO

SCENE.   *Dining-room of the Miller home—a little after six o'clock in the evening of the same day.*

The room is much too small for the medium-priced, formidable dining-room set, especially now when all the leaves of the table are in.   At left, toward rear, is a double doorway with sliding doors and portières leading into the back parlour.   In the rear wall, left, is the door to the pantry.   At the right of door is the china closet with its display of the family cut glass and fancy china.   In the right wall are two windows looking out on a side lawn.   In front of the windows is a heavy, ugly sideboard with three pieces of old silver on its top. In the left wall, extreme front, is a screen door opening on a side porch.   A dark rug covers most of the floor. The table, with a chair at each end, left and right, three chairs on the far side, facing front, and two on the near side, their backs to front, takes up most of the available space.   The walls are papered in a sombre brown and dark-red design.

Mrs. Miller is supervising and helping the second girl, Norah, in the setting of the table.   Norah is a clumsy, heavy-handed, heavy-footed, long-jawed, beamingly good-natured young Irish girl—a " greenhorn."

MRS. MILLER.   I really think you better put on the lights, Norah.   It's getting so cloudy out, and this pesky room is so dark, anyway.

45

NORAH. Yes, Mum. (*She stretches awkwardly over the table to reach the chandelier that is suspended from the middle of the ceiling and manages to turn one light on—scornfully.*) Arrah, the contraption!

MRS. MILLER (*worriedly*). Careful!

NORAH. Careful as can be, Mum. (*But in moving around to reach the next bulb she jars heavily against the table.*)

MRS. MILLER. There! I knew it! I do wish you'd watch—— !

NORAH (*a flustered appeal in her voice.*) Arrah, what have I done wrong now?

MRS. MILLER (*draws a deep breath—then sighs helplessly*). Oh, nothing. Never mind the rest of the lights. You might as well go out in the kitchen and wait until I ring.

NORAH (*relieved and cheerful again*). Yes, Mum. (*She starts for the pantry.*)

MRS. MILLER. But there's one thing—— (*Norah turns apprehensively.*) No, two things—things I've told you over and over, but you always forget. Don't pass the plates on the wrong side at dinner to-night, and do be careful not to let that pantry door slam behind you. Now you will try to remember, won't you?

NORAH. Yes, Mum.

> (*She goes into the pantry and shuts the door behind her with exaggerated care as Mrs. Miller watches her apprehensively. Mrs. Miller sighs and reaches up with difficulty and turns on another of the four lights in the chandelier. As she is doing so, Lily enters from the back parlour.*)

LILY. Here, let me do that, Essie. I'm taller. You'll only strain yourself. (*She quickly lights the other two bulbs.*)

MRS. MILLER (*gratefully*). Thank you, Lily. It's a stretch for me, I'm getting so fat.

LILY. But where's Norah ? Why didn't she——— ?

MRS. MILLER (*exasperatedly*). Oh, that girl ! Don't talk about her ! She'll be the death of me ! She's that thick, you honestly wouldn't believe it possible.

LILY (*smiling*). Why, what did she do now ?

MRS. MILLER. Oh, nothing. She means all right.

LILY. Anything else I can do, Essie ?

MRS. MILLER. Well, she's got the table all wrong. We'll have to reset it. But you're always helping me. It isn't fair to ask you—in your vacation. You need your rest after teaching a pack of wild Indians of kids all year.

LILY (*beginning to help with the table*). You know I love to help. It makes me feel I'm some use in this house instead of just sponging———

MRS. MILLER (*indignantly*). Sponging ! You pay, don't you ?

LILY. Almost nothing. And you and Nat only take that little to make me feel better about living with you. (*Forcing a smile.*) I don't see how you stand me—having a cranky old maid around all the time.

MRS. MILLER. What nonsense you talk ! As if Nat and I weren't only too tickled to death to have you ! Lily Miller, I've no patience with you when you go on like that. We've been over this a thousand times before, and still you go on ! Crazy, that's what it is ! (*She changes the subject abruptly.*) What time's it getting to be ?

LILY (*looking at her watch*). Quarter past six.

MRS. MILLER. I do hope those men folks aren't going to be late for dinner. (*She sighs.*) But I suppose with that darned Sachem Club picnic it's more likely than not. (*Lily looks worried, and sighs. Mrs. Miller gives her a quick side glance.*) I see you've got your new dress on.

LILY (*embarrassedly*). Yes, I thought—if Sid's taking me to the fireworks—I ought to spruce up a little.

MRS. MILLER (*looking away*). Hmm. (*A pause—then she says with an effort to be casual :*) You mustn't mind if Sid comes home feeling a bit—gay. I expect Nat to—and we'll have to listen to all those old stories of his about when he was a boy. You know what those picnics are, and Sid'd be running into all his old friends.

LILY (*agitatedly*). I don't think he will—this time—not after his promise.

MRS. MILLER (*avoiding looking at her*). I know. But men are weak. (*Then quickly.*) That was a good notion of Nat's, getting Sid the job on the Waterbury " Standard." All he ever needed was to get away from the rut he was in here. He's the kind that's the victim of his friends. He's easily led—but there's no real harm in him, you know that. (*Lily keeps silent, her eyes downcast. Mrs. Miller goes on meaningly.*) He's making good money in Waterbury, too—thirty-five a week. He's in a better position to get married than he ever was.

LILY (*stiffly*). Well, I hope he finds a woman who's willing—though after he's through with his betting on horse-races, and dice, and playing Kelly pool, there won't be much left for a wife—even if there was nothing else he spent his money on.

MRS. MILLER. Oh, he'd give up all that—for the right woman. (*Suddenly she comes directly to the point.*) Lily, why don't you change your mind and marry Sid and reform him ? You love him and always have——

LILY (*stiffly*). I can't love a man who drinks.

MRS. MILLER. You can't fool me. I know darned well you love him. And he loves you and always has.

LILY. Never enough to stop drinking for. (*Cutting off Mrs. Miller's reply.*) No, it's no good in your talking, Essie. We've been over this a thousand times before and I'll always feel the same as long as Sid's the same. If he gave me proof he'd—but even then I don't believe I could. It's sixteen years since I broke off our engagement, but what made me break it off is as clear to me to-day as it was then. It was what he'd be liable to do now to anyone who married him—his taking up with bad women.

MRS. MILLER (*protests half-heartedly*). But he's always sworn he got raked into that party and never had anything to do with those harlots.

LILY. Well, I don't believe him—didn't then and don't now. I do believe he didn't deliberately plan to, but—— Oh, it's no good talking, Essie. What's done is done. But you know how much I like Sid—in spite of everything. I know he was just born to be what he is—irresponsible, never meaning to harm but harming in spite of himself. But don't talk to me about marrying him—because I never could.

MRS. MILLER (*angrily*). He's a dumb fool—a stupid dumb fool, that's what he is !

LILY (*quietly*). No. He's just Sid.

MRS. MILLER. It's a shame for you—a measly shame —you that would have made such a wonderful wife for any man—that ought to have your own home and children !

LILY (*winces but puts her arm around her affectionately—gently*). Now don't you go feeling sorry for me. I won't have that. Here I am, thanks to your and Nat's kindness, with the best home in the world ; and as for the children, I feel the same love for yours as if they were mine, and I didn't have the pain of bearing them. And then there are all the boys and girls I teach every year. I like to feel I'm a sort of second mother to them and helping them to grow up to be good men and women. So I don't feel such a useless old maid, after all.

MRS. MILLER (*kisses her impulsively—her voice husky*). You're a good woman, Lily—too good for the rest of us. (*She turns away, wiping a tear furtively—then abruptly changing the subject.*) Good gracious, if I'm not forgetting one of the most important things ! I've got to warn that Tommy against giving me away to Nat about the fish. He knows, because I had to send him to market for it, and he's liable to burst out laughing——

LILY. Laughing about what ?

MRS. MILLER (*guiltily*). Well, I've never told you, because it seemed sort of a sneaking trick, but you know how Nat carries on about not being able to eat bluefish.

LILY. I know he says there's a certain oil in it that poisons him.

MRS. MILLER (*chuckling*). Poisons him, nothing ! He's been eating bluefish for years—only I tell him each time it's weakfish. We're having it to-night—and I've got to warn that young imp to keep his face straight.

LILY (*laughing*). Aren't you ashamed, Essie !

MRS. MILLER. Not much, I'm not ! I like bluefish ! (*She laughs.*) Where is Tommy ? In the sitting-room ?

LILY. No, Richard's there alone. I think Tommy's out on the piazza with Mildred.

> (*Mrs. Miller bustles out through the back parlour. As soon as she is gone, the smile fades from Lily's lips. Her face grows sad and she again glances nervously at her watch. Richard appears from the back parlour, moving in an aimless way. His face wears a set expression of bitter gloom ; he exudes tragedy. For Richard, after his first outburst of grief and humiliation, has begun to take a masochistic satisfaction in his great sorrow, especially in the concern which it arouses in the family circle. On seeing his aunt, he gives her a dark look and turns and is about to stalk back toward the sitting-room when she speaks to him pityingly.*)

Feel any better, Richard ?

RICHARD (*sombrely*). I'm all right, Aunt Lily. You mustn't worry about me.

LILY (*going to him*). But I do worry about you. I hate to see you so upset.

RICHARD. It doesn't matter. Nothing matters.

LILY (*puts her arm around him sympathetically*). You

51

really mustn't let yourself take it so seriously. You know, something happens and things like that come up, and we think there's no hope——

RICHARD. Things like what come up ?

LILY. What's happened between you and Muriel.

RICHARD (*with disdain*). Oh, her ! I wasn't even thinking about her. I was thinking about life.

LILY. But then—if we really, *really* love—why, then something else is bound to happen soon that changes everything again, and it's all as it was before the misunderstanding, and everything works out all right in the end. That's the way it is with life.

RICHARD (*with a tragic sneer*). Life ! Life is a joke ! And everything comes out all wrong in the end !

LILY (*a little shocked*). You mustn't talk that way. But I know you don't mean it.

RICHARD. I do too mean it ! You can have your silly optimism, if you like, Aunt Lily. But don't ask me to be so blind. I'm a pessimist ! (*Then with an air of cruel cynicism.*) As for Muriel, that's all dead and past. I was only kidding her, anyway, just to have a little fun, and she took it seriously, like a fool. (*He forces a cruel smile to his lips.*) You know what they say about women and trolley cars, Aunt Lily : there's always another one along in a minute.

LILY (*really shocked this time*). I don't like you when you say such horrible, cynical things. It isn't nice.

RICHARD. Nice ! That's all you women think of ! I'm proud to be a cynic. It's the only thing you can be when you really face life. I suppose you think I ought to be heart-broken about Muriel—a little coward that's afraid to say her soul's her own, and keeps tied to her father's apron strings ! Well, not for mine ! There's plenty of other fish in the sea ! (*As he is finishing, his mother comes back through the back parlour.*)

MRS. MILLER. Why, hello. You here, Richard ? Getting hungry, I suppose ?

RICHARD (*indignantly*). I'm not hungry a bit ! That's all you think of, Ma—food !

MRS. MILLER. Well, I must say I've never noticed you to hang back at mealtimes. (*To Lily.*) What's that he was saying about fish in the sea ?

LILY (*smiling*). He says he's through with Muriel now.

MRS. MILLER (*tartly—giving her son a rebuking look*). She's through with him, he means ! The idea of your sending a nice girl like her things out of those indecent books !

(*Deeply offended, Richard disdains to reply but stalks woundedly to the screen door at left, front, and puts a hand on the knob.*)

Where are you going ?

RICHARD (*quotes from " Candida " in a hollow voice*). " Out, then, into the night with me ! "

(*He stalks out, slamming the door behind him.*)

MRS. MILLER (*calls*). Well, don't you go far, 'cause dinner'll be ready in a minute, and I'm not coming running after you ! (*She turns to Lily with a chuckle.*) Goodness, that boy ! He ought to be on the stage ! (*She mimics.*) " Out—into the night "—and it isn't even dark yet ! He got that out of one of those books,

I suppose. Do you know, I'm actually grateful to old Dave McComber for putting an end to his nonsense with Muriel. I never did approve of Richard getting so interested in girls. He's not old enough for such silliness. Why, seems to me it was only yesterday he was still a baby. (*She sighs—then matter-of-factly.*) Well, nothing to do now till those men turn up. No use standing here like gawks. We might as well go in the sitting-room and be comfortable.

LILY (*the nervous, worried note in her voice again*). Yes, we might as well. (*They go out through the back parlour. They have no sooner disappeared than the screen door is opened cautiously and Richard comes back in the room.*)

RICHARD (*stands inside the door, looking after them— quotes bitterly*). " They do not know the secret in the poet's heart." (*He comes nearer the table and surveys it, especially the cut-glass dish containing olives, with contempt and mutters disdainfully.*) Food !

(*But the dish of olives seems to fascinate him and presently he has approached nearer, and stealthily lifts a couple and crams them into his mouth. He is just reaching out for more when the pantry door is opened slightly and Norah peers in.*)

NORAH. Mister Dick, you thief, lave them olives alone, or the missus'll be swearing it was me at them !

RICHARD (*draws back his hand as if he had been stung— too flustered to be anything but guilty boy for a second*). I—I wasn't eating——

NORAH. Oho, no, of course not, divil fear you, you was only feeling their pulse ! (*Then warningly.*) Mind what I'm saying now, or I'll have to tell on you to protect me good name !

(She draws back into the pantry, closing the door. Richard stands, a prey to feelings of bitterest humiliation and seething revolt against everyone and everything. A low whistle comes from just outside the porch door. He starts. Then a masculine voice calls: " Hey, Dick." He goes over to the screen door grumpily—then as he recognizes the owner of the voice, his own as he answers becomes respectful and admiring.)

RICHARD. Oh, hello, Wint. Come on in.

(He opens the door and Wint Selby enters and stands just inside the door. Selby is nineteen, a classmate of Arthur's at Yale. He is a typical, good-looking college boy of the period, not the athletic but the hell-raising sport type. He is tall, blond, dressed in extreme collegiate cut.)

WINT *(as he enters—warningly, in a low tone)*. Keep it quiet, Kid. I don't want the folks to know I'm here. Tell Art I want to see him a second—on the Q.T.

RICHARD. Can't. He's up at the Rands'—won't be home before ten, anyway.

WINT *(irritably)*. Damn ! I thought he'd be here for dinner. *(More irritably.)* Hell, that gums the works for fair !

RICHARD *(ingratiatingly)*. What is it, Wint ? Can't I help ?

WINT *(gives him an appraising glance)*. I might tell you, if you can keep your face shut.

RICHARD. I can.

WINT. Well, I ran into a couple of swift babies from

New Haven this after. and I dated them up for to-night, thinking I could catch Art. But now it's too late to get anyone else and I'll have to pass it up. I'm nearly broke and I can't afford to blow them both to drinks.

RICHARD (*with shy eagerness*). I've got eleven dollars saved up. I could loan you some.

WINT (*surveys him appreciatively*). Say, you're a good sport. (*Then shaking his head.*) Nix, Kid, I don't want to borrow your money. (*Then getting an idea.*) But say, have you got anything on for to-night ?

RICHARD. No.

WINT. Want to come along with me ? (*Then quickly.*) I'm not trying to lead you astray, understand. But it'll be a help if you would just sit around with Belle and feed her a few drinks while I'm off with Edith. (*He winks.*) See what I mean ? You don't have to do anything, not even take a glass of beer—unless you want to.

RICHARD (*boastfully*). Aw, what do you think I am—a rube ?

WINT. You mean you're game for anything that's doing ?

RICHARD. Sure I am !

WINT. Ever been out with any girls—I mean, real swift ones that there's something doing with, not these dead Janes around here ?

RICHARD (*lies boldly*). Aw, what do you think ? Sure I have !

WINT. Ever drink anything besides sodas ?

RICHARD. Sure. Lots of times. Beer and sloe-gin fizz and—Manhattans.

56

WINT (*impressed*). Hell, you know more than I thought. (*Then considering.*) Can you fix it so your folks won't get wise ? I don't want your old man coming after me. You can get back by half-past ten or eleven, though, all right. Think you can cook up some lie to cover that ? (*As Richard hesitates—encouraging him.*) Ought to be easy—on the Fourth.

RICHARD. Sure. Don't worry about that.

WINT. But you've got to keep your face closed about this, you hear ?—to Art and everybody else. I tell you straight, I wouldn't ask you to come if I wasn't in a hole —and if I didn't know you were coming down to Yale next year, and didn't think you're giving me the straight goods about having been around before. I don't want to lead you astray.

RICHARD (*scornfully*). Aw, I told you that was silly.

WINT. Well, you be at the Pleasant Beach Hotel at half-past nine then. Come in the back room. And don't forget to grab some cloves to take the booze off your breath.

RICHARD. Aw, I know what to do.

WINT. See you later, then. (*He starts out and is just about to close the door when he thinks of something.*) And say, I'll say you're a Harvard freshman, and you back me up. They don't know a damn thing about Harvard. I don't want them thinking I'm travelling around with any high-school kid.

RICHARD. Sure. That's easy.

WINT. So long, then. You better beat it right after your dinner while you've got a chance, and hang around until it's time. Watch your step, Kid.

RICHARD. So long. (*The door closes behind Wint. Richard stands for a moment, a look of bitter, defiant rebellion coming over his face, and mutters to himself.*) I'll show her she can't treat me the way she's done ! I'll show them all !

> (*Then the front door is heard slamming, and a moment later Tommy rushes in from the back parlour.*)

TOMMY. Where's Ma ?

RICHARD (*surlily*). In the sitting-room. Where did you think, Bonehead ?

TOMMY. Pa and Uncle Sid are coming. Mid and I saw them from the front piazza. Gee, I'm glad. I'm awful hungry, ain't you ? (*He rushes out through the back parlour, calling* :) Ma ! They're coming ! Let's have dinner quick ! (*A moment later Mrs. Miller appears from the back parlour accompanied by Tommy, who keeps insisting urgently* :) Gee, but I'm awful hungry, Ma !

MRS. MILLER. I know. You always are. You've got a tape-worm, that's what I think.

TOMMY. Have we got lobsters, Ma ? Gee, I love lobsters.

MRS. MILLER. Yes, we've got lobsters. And fish. You remember what I told you about that fish. (*He snickers.*) Now, do be quiet, Tommy ! (*Then with a teasing smile at Richard* :) Well, I'm glad to see you've got back out of the night, Richard.

> (*He scowls and turns his back on her. Lily appears through the back parlour, nervous and apprehensive. As she does so, from the front yard*

Sid's voice is heard singing " Poor John ! "
Mrs. Miller shakes her head forebodingly—
but, so great is the comic spell for her even in her
brother's voice, a humorous smile hovers at the
corners of her lips.)

Mmm ! Mmm ! Lily, I'm afraid——

LILY (*bitterly*). Yes, I might have known.

(*Mildred runs in through the back parlour. She is*
laughing to herself a bit shamefacedly. She
rushes to her mother.)

MILDRED. Ma, Uncle Sid's—— (*She whispers in*
her ear.)

MRS. MILLER. Never mind ! You shouldn't notice
such things—at your age ! And don't you encourage
him by laughing at his foolishness, you hear !

TOMMY. You needn't whisper, Mid. Think I don't
know ? Uncle Sid's soused again.

MRS. MILLER (*shakes him by the arm indignantly*). You
be quiet ! Did I ever ! You're getting too smart !
(*Gives him a push.*) Go to your place and sit right
down and not another word out of you !

TOMMY (*aggrieved—rubbing his arm as he goes to his*
place). Aw, Ma !

MRS. MILLER. And you sit down, Richard and Mildred. You better, too, Lily. We'll get him right in
here and get some food in him. He'll be all right then.

(*Richard, preserving the pose of the bitter, dis-*
illusioned pessimist, sits down in his place in
the chair at right of the two whose backs face

59

front. Mildred takes the other chair facing back, at his left. Tommy has already slid into the end chair at right of those at the rear of table facing front. Lily sits in the one of those at left, by the head of the table, leaving the middle one [Sid's] vacant. While they are doing this, the front screen door is heard slamming and Miller and Sid's laughing voices, raised as they come in and for a moment after, then suddenly cautiously lowered. Mrs. Miller goes to the entrance to the back parlour and calls peremptorily.)

You come right in here ! Don't stop to wash up or anything. Dinner's coming right on the table.

MILLER'S VOICE (*jovially*). All right, Essie. Here we are ! Here we are !

MRS. MILLER (*goes to pantry door, opens it and calls*). All right, Norah. You can bring in the soup.

(She comes back to the back-parlour entrance just as Miller enters. He isn't drunk by any means. He is just mellow and benignly ripened. His face is one large, smiling, happy beam of utter appreciation of life. All's right with the world, so satisfyingly right that he becomes sentimentally moved even to think of it.)

MILLER. Here we are, Essie ! Right on the dot ! Here we are !

(He pulls her to him and gives her a smacking kiss on the ear as she jerks her head away. Mildred and Tommy giggle. Richard holds rigidly aloof and disdainful, his brooding gaze fixed on his plate. Lily forces a smile.)

MRS. MILLER (*pulling away—embarrassedly, almost blushing*). Don't, you Crazy ! (*Then recovering herself—tartly.*) So I see, you're here ! And if I didn't, you've told me four times already !

MILLER (*beamingly*). Now, Essie, don't be critical. Don't be carpingly critical. Good news can stand repeating, can't it ? 'Course it can !

> (*He slaps her jovially on her fat buttocks. Tommy and Mildred roar with glee. And Norah, who has just entered from the pantry with a huge tureen of soup in her hands, almost drops it as she explodes in a merry guffaw.*)

MRS. MILLER (*scandalized*). Nat ! Aren't you ashamed !

MILLER. Couldn't resist it ! Just simply couldn't resist it !

> (*Norah, still standing with the soup tureen held out stiffly in front of her, again guffaws.*)

MRS. MILLER (*turns on her with outraged indignation*). Norah ! Bring that soup here this minute ! (*She stalks with stiff dignity toward her place at the foot of the table, right.*)

NORAH (*guiltily*). Yes, Mum. (*She brings the soup around the head of the table, passing Miller.*)

MILLER (*jovially*). Why, hello, Norah !

MRS. MILLER. Nat ! (*She sits down stiffly at the foot of the table.*)

NORAH (*rebuking him familiarly*). Arrah now, don't be making me laugh and getting me into trouble !

MRS. MILLER. Norah !

NORAH (*a bit resentfully*). Yes, Mum. Here I am. (*She sets the soup tureen down with a thud in front of Mrs. Miller and passes around the other side, squeezing with difficulty between the china closet and the backs of chairs at the rear of the table.*)

MRS. MILLER. Tommy ! Stop spinning your napkin ring ! How often have I got to tell you ? Mildred ! Sit up straight in your chair ! Do you want to grow up a humpback ? Richard ! Take your elbows off the table !

MILLER (*coming to his place at the head of the table, rubbing his hands together genially*). Well, well, well. Well, well, well. It's good to be home again.

(*Norah exits into the pantry and lets the door slam with a bang behind her.*)

MRS. MILLER (*jumps*). Oh ! (*Then exasperatedly.*) Nat, I do wish you wouldn't encourage that stupid girl by talking to her, when I'm doing my best to train——

MILLER (*beamingly*). All right, Essie. Your word is law ! (*Then laughingly.*) We did have the darndest fun to-day ! And Sid was the life of that picnic ! You ought to have heard him ! Honestly, he had that crowd just rolling on the ground and splitting their sides ! He ought to be on the stage.

MRS. MILLER (*as Norah comes back with a dish of saltines —begins ladling soup into the stack of plates before her*). He ought to be at this table eating something to sober him up, that's what he ought to be ! (*She calls.*) Sid ! You come right in here ! (*Then to Norah, handing her a*

soup plate.) Here, Norah. (*Norah begins passing soup.*)
Sit down, Nat, for goodness' sakes. Start eating, everybody. Don't wait for me. You know I've given up
soup.

MILLER (*sits down but bends forward to call to his wife in a
confidential tone*). Essie—Sid's sort of embarrassed about
coming—I mean I'm afraid he's a little bit—not too
much, you understand—but he met such a lot of friends
and—well, you know, don't be hard on him. Fourth of
July is like Christmas—comes but once a year. Don't
pretend to notice, eh ? And don't you kids, you hear !
And don't you, Lily. He's scared of you.

LILY (*with stiff meekness*). Very well, Nat.

MILLER (*beaming again—calls*). All right, Sid. The
coast's clear. (*He begins to absorb his soup ravenously.*)
Good soup, Essie ! Good soup !

> (*A moment later Sid makes his entrance from the
> back parlour. He is in a condition that can
> best be described as blurry. His movements
> have a hazy uncertainty about them. His
> shiny fat face is one broad, blurred, Puckish,
> naughty-boy grin ; his eyes have a blurred,
> wondering vagueness. As he enters he makes
> a solemnly intense effort to appear casual and
> dead, cold sober. He waves his hand aim-
> lessly and speaks with a silly gravity.*)

SID. Good evening. (*They all answer " Good evening," their eyes on their plates. He makes his way vaguely
toward his place, continuing his grave effort at conversation.*)
Beautiful evening. I never remember seeing—more
beautiful sunset. (*He bumps vaguely into Lily's chair as*

he attempts to pass behind her—immediately he is all grave politeness.) Sorry—sorry, Lily—deeply sorry.

LILY (*her eyes on her plate—stiffly*). It's all right.

SID (*manages to get into his chair at last—mutters to himself*). Wha' was I sayin' ? Oh, sunsets. But why butt in ? Hasn't sun—perfect right to set ? Mind y'r own business. (*He pauses thoughtfully, considering this—then looks around from face to face, fixing each with a vague, blurred, wondering look, as if some deep puzzle were confronting him. Then suddenly he grins mistily and nods with satisfaction.*) And there you are ! Am I right ?

MILLER (*humouring him*). Right.

SID. Right ! (*He is silent, studying his soup plate, as if it were some strange enigma. Finally he looks up and regards his sister and asks with wondering amazement.*) Soup ?

MRS. MILLER. Of course, it's soup. What did you think it was ? And you hurry up and eat it.

SID (*again regards his soup with astonishment*). Well ! (*Then suddenly.*) Well, all right then ! Soup be it ! (*He picks up his spoon and begins to eat, but after two tries in which he finds it difficult to locate his mouth, he addresses the spoon plaintively*). Spoon, is this any way to treat a pal ? (*Then suddenly comically angry, putting the spoon down with a bang.*) Down with spoons ! (*He raises his soup plate and declaims:*) " We'll drink to the dead already, and hurrah for the next who dies." (*Bowing solemnly to right and left.*) Your good health, ladies *and* gents.

(*He starts drinking the soup. Miller guffaws and
Mildred and Tommy giggle. Even Richard*

*forgets his melancholy and snickers, and Mrs.
Miller conceals a smile. Only Lily remains
stiff and silent.)*

MRS. MILLER (*with forced severity*).   Sid !

SID (*peers at her muzzily, lowering the soup plate a little
from his lips*).   Eh ?

MRS. MILLER.   Oh, nothing.   Never mind.

SID (*solemnly offended*).   Are you—publicly rebuking
me before assembled——— ?   Isn't soup liquid ?   Aren't
liquids drunk ?   (*Then considering this to himself.*)   What
if they are drunk ?   It's a good man's failing.   (*He
again peers mistily about at the company.*)   Am I right or
wrong ?

MRS. MILLER.   Hurry up and finish your soup, and
stop talking nonsense !

SID (*turning to her—again offendedly*.   Oh, no, Essie,
if I ever so far forget myself as to drink a leg of lamb,
then you might have some—excuse for———   Just think
of waste effort eating soup with spoons—fifty gruelling
lifts per plate—billions of soup-eaters on globe—why,
it's simply staggering !   (*Then darkly to himself.*)   No
more spoons for me !   If I want to develop my biceps,
I'll buy Sandow Exerciser !   (*He drinks the rest of his
soup in a gulp and beams around at the company, suddenly
all happiness again.*)   Am I right, folks ?

MILLER (*who has been choking with laughter*).   Haw,
haw !   You're right, Sid.

SID (*peers at him blurredly and shakes his head sadly*).
Poor old Nat !   Always wrong—but heart of gold,
heart of purest gold.   And drunk again, I regret to

note. Sister, my heart bleeds for you and your poor fatherless chicks !

MRS. MILLER (*restraining a giggle—severely*). Sid ! Do shut up for a minute ! Pass me your soup plates, everybody. If we wait for that girl to take them, we'll be here all night.

> (*They all pass their plates, which Mrs. Miller stacks up and then puts on the sideboard. As she is doing this, Norah appears from the pantry with a platter of broiled fish. She is just about to place these before Miller when Sid catches her eye mistily and rises to his feet, making her a deep, uncertain bow.*)

SID (*rapidly*). Ah, Sight for Sore Eyes, my beautiful Macushla, my star-eyed Mavourneen——

MRS. MILLER. Sid !

NORAH (*immensely pleased—gives him an arch, flirtatious glance*). Ah sure, Mister Sid, it's you that have kissed the Blarney Stone, when you've a drop taken !

MRS. MILLER (*outraged*). Norah ! Put down that fish !

NORAH (*flusteredly*). Yes, Mum. (*She attempts to put the fish down hastily before Miller, but her eyes are fixed nervously on Mrs. Miller and she gives Miller a nasty swipe on the side of the head with the edge of the dish.*)

MILLER. Ouch !

> (*The children, even Richard, explode into laughter.*)

NORAH (*almost lets the dish fall*). Oh, glory be to God ! Is it hurted you are ?

MILLER (*rubbing his head—good-naturedly*). No, no harm done. Only careful, Norah, careful.

NORAH (*gratefully*). Yes, sorr. (*She thumps down the dish in front of him with a sigh of relief.*)

SID (*who is still standing—with drunken gravity*). Careful, Mavourneen, careful ! You might have hit him some place besides the head. Always aim at his head, remember—so as not to worry us.

(*Again the children explode. Also Norah. Even Lily suddenly lets out an hysterical giggle and is furious with herself for doing so.*)

LILY. I'm so sorry, Nat. I didn't mean to laugh. (*Turning on Sid furiously.*) Will you please sit down and stop making a fool of yourself !

(*Sid gives her a hurt, mournful look and then sinks meekly down on his chair.*)

NORAH (*grinning cheerfully, gives Lily a reassuring pat on the back*). Ah, Miss Lily, don't mind him. He's only under the influence. Sure, there's no harm in him at all.

MRS. MILLER. Norah !

(*Norah exits hastily into the pantry, letting the door slam with a crash behind her. There is silence for a moment as Miller serves the fish and it is passed around. Norah comes back with the vegetables and disappears again, and these are dished out.*)

MILLER (*is about to take his first bite—stops suddenly and asks his wife*). This isn't, by any chance, bluefish, is it, my dear ?

MRS. MILLER (*with a warning glance at Tommy*). Of

67

course not. You know we never have bluefish, on account of you.

MILLER (*addressing the table now with the gravity of a man confessing his strange peculiarities*). Yes, I regret to say, there's a certain peculiar oil in bluefish that invariably poisons me.

> (*At this, Tommy cannot stand it any more but explodes into laughter. Mrs. Miller, after a helpless glance at him, follows suit; then Lily goes off into uncontrollable, hysterical laughter, and Richard and Mildred are caught in the contagion. Miller looks around at them with a weak smile, his dignity now ruffled a bit.*)

Well, I must say I don't see what's so darned funny about my being poisoned.

SID (*peers around him—then with drunken cunning*). Aha ! Nat, I suspect—plot ! This fish looks blue to me—very blue—in fact despondent, desperate, and—— (*He points his fork dramatically, at Mrs. Miller.*) See how guilty she looks—a ver—veritable Lucretia Georgia ! Can it be this woman has been slowly poisoning you all these years ? And how well—you've stood it ! What iron constitution ! Even now, when you are invariably at death's door, I can't believe——

> (*Everyone goes off into uncontrollable laughter.*)

MILLER (*grumpily*). Oh, give us a rest, you darned fool ! A joke's a joke, but—— (*He addresses his wife in a wounded tone.*) Is this true, Essie ?

MRS. MILLER (*wiping the tears from her eyes—defiantly*). Yes, it is true, if you must know, and you'd never have suspected it, if it weren't for that darned Tommy, and

68

Sid poking his nose in. You've eaten bluefish for years and thrived on it and it's all nonsense about that peculiar oil.

MILLER (*deeply offended*). Kindly allow me to know my own constitution ! Now I think of it, I've felt upset afterwards every damned time we've had fish ! (*He pushes his plate away from him with proud renunciation.*) I can't eat this.

MRS. MILLER (*insultingly matter-of-fact*). Well, don't then. There's lots of lobster coming and you can fill up on that.

(*Richard suddenly bursts out laughing again.*)

MILLER (*turns to him caustically*). You seem in a merry mood, Richard. I thought you were the original of the Heart Bowed Down to-day.

SID (*with mock condolence*). Never mind, Dick. Let them—scoff ! What can they understand about girls whose hair sizzchels, whose lips are fireworks, whose eyes are red-hot sparks——

MILDRED (*laughing*). Is that what he wrote to Muriel ? (*Turning to her brother.*) You silly goat, you !

RICHARD (*surlily*). Aw, shut up, Mid. What do I care about her ? I'll show all of you how much I care !

MRS. MILLER. Pass your plates as soon as you're through, everybody. I've rung for the lobster. And that's all. You don't get any dessert or tea after lobster, you know.

(*Norah appears bearing a platter of cold boiled lobsters which she sets before Miller, and disappears.*)

TOMMY.   Gee, I love lobster !

> (*Miller puts one on each plate, and they are passed around and everyone starts in pulling the cracked shells apart.*)

MILLER (*feeling more cheerful after a couple of mouthfuls —determining to give the conversation another turn, says to his daughter*).   Have a good time at the beach, Mildred ?

MILDRED.   Oh, fine, Pa, thanks.   The water was wonderful and warm.

MILLER.   Swim far ?

MILDRED.   Yes, for me.   But that isn't so awful far.

MILLER.   Well, you ought to be a good swimmer, if you take after me.   I used to be a regular water-rat when I was a boy.   I'll have to go down to the beach with you one of these days—though I'd be rusty, not having been in in all these years. (*The reminiscent look comes into his eyes of one about to embark on an oft-told tale of childhood adventure.*)   You know, speaking of swimming, I never go down to that beach but what it calls to mind the day I and Red Sisk went in swimming there and I saved his life.

> (*By this time the family are beginning to exchange amused, guilty glances.   They all know what is coming.*)

SID (*with a sly, blurry wink around*).   Ha !   Now we —have it again !

MILLER (*turning on him*).   Have what ?

SID.   Nothing—go on with your swimming—don't mind me.

MILLER (*glares at him—but immediately is overcome by the reminiscent mood again*).   Red Sisk—his father kept a blacksmith shop where the Union Market is now—we kids called him Red because he had the darndest reddest crop of hair——

SID (*as if he were talking to his plate*).   Remarkable ! —the curious imagination—of little children.

MRS. MILLER (*as she sees Miller about to explode—interposes tactfully*).   Sid !   Eat your lobster and shut up ! Go on, Nat.

MILLER (*gives Sid a withering look—then is off again*). Well, as I was saying, Red and I went swimming that day.   Must have been—let me see—Red was fourteen, bigger and older than me, I was only twelve—forty-five years ago—wasn't a single house down there then —but there was a stake out where the whistling buoy is now, about a mile out.

> (*Tommy, who has been having difficulty restraining himself, lets out a stifled giggle.   Miller bends a frowning gaze on him.*)

One more sound out of you, young man, and you'll leave the table !

MRS. MILLER (*quickly interposing, trying to stave off the story*).   Do eat your lobster, Nat.   You didn't have any fish, you know.

MILLER (*not liking the reminder—pettishly*).   Well, if I'm going to be interrupted every second anyway——

(*He turns to his lobster and chews in silence for a moment.*)

MRS. MILLER (*trying to switch the subject*).   How's Anne's mother's rheumatism, Mildred ?

MILDRED. Oh, she's much better, Ma. She was in wading to-day. She says salt water's the only thing that really helps her bunion.

MRS. MILLER. Mildred ! Where are your manners ? At the table's no place to speak of——

MILLER (*fallen into the reminiscent obsession again*). Well, as I was saying, there was I and Red, and he dared me to race him out to the stake and back. Well, I didn't let anyone dare me in those days. I was a spunky kid. So I said all right and we started out. We swam and swam and were pretty evenly matched ; though, as I've said, he was bigger and older than me, but finally I drew ahead. I was going along easy, with lots in reserve, not a bit tired, when suddenly I heard a sort of gasp from behind me—like this—" help ! " (*He imitates. Everyone's eyes are firmly fixed on their plates, except Sid's.*) And I turned and there was Red, his face all pinched and white, and he says weakly : " Help, Nat ! I got a cramp in my leg ! " Well, I don't mind telling you I got mighty scared. I didn't know what to do.. Then suddenly I thought of the pile. If I could pull him to that, I could hang on to him till someone'd notice us. But the pile was still—well, I calculate it must have been two hundred feet away.

SID. Two hundred and fifty !

MILLER (*in confusion*). What's that ?

SID. Two hundred *and* fifty ! I've taken down the distance every time you've saved Red's life for thirty years and the mean average to that pile is two hundred and fifty feet ! (*There is a burst of laughter from around the table. Sid continues complainingly.*) Why didn't you let that Red drown, anyway, Nat ? I never knew him but I know I'd never have liked him.

MILLER (*really hurt, forces a feeble smile to his lips and pretends to be a good sport about it*). Well, guess you're right, Sid. Guess I have told that one too many times and bored everyone. But it's a good true story for kids because it illustrates the danger of being foolhardy in the water——

MRS. MILLER (*sensing the hurt in his tone, comes to his rescue*). Of course it's a good story—and you tell it whenever you've a mind to. And you, Sid, if you were in any responsible state, I'd give you a good piece of my mind for teasing Nat like that.

MILLER (*with a sad, self-pitying smile at his wife*). Getting old, I guess, Mother—getting to repeat myself. Someone ought to stop me.

MRS. MILLER. No such thing ! You're as young as you ever were. (*She turns on Sid again angrily.*) You eat your lobster and maybe it'll keep your mouth shut !

SID (*after a few chews—irrepressibly*). Lobster ! Did you know, Tommy, your Uncle Sid is the man invented lobster ? Fact ! One day—when I was building the Pyramids—took a day off and just dashed off lobster. He was bigger'n' older than me and he had the darndest reddest crop of hair but I dashed him off just the same ! Am I right, Nat ? (*Then suddenly in the tones of a side-show barker.*) Ladies *and* Gents——

MRS. MILLER. Mercy sakes ! Can't you shut up ?

SID. In this cage you see the lobster. You will not believe me, ladies *and* gents, but it's a fact that this interesting bivalve only makes love to his mate once in every thousand years—but, dearie me, how he does enjoy it !

> (*The children roar. Lily and Mrs. Miller laugh in spite of themselves—then look embarrassed. Miller guffaws—then suddenly grows shocked.*)

MILLER. Careful, Sid, careful. Remember you're at home.

TOMMY (*suddenly in a hoarse whisper to his mother, with an awed glance of admiration at his uncle*). Ma ! Look at him ! He's eating that claw, shells and all !

MRS. MILLER (*horrified*). Sid, do you want to kill yourself ? Take it away from him, Lily !

SID (*with great dignity*). But I prefer the shells. All famous epicures prefer the shells—to the less delicate, coarser meat. It's the same with clams. Unless I eat the shells there is a certain, peculiar oil that invariably poisons—— Am I right, Nat ?

MILLER (*good-naturedly*). You seem to be getting a lot of fun kidding me. Go ahead, then. I don't mind.

MRS. MILLER. He better go right up to bed for a while, that's what he better do.

SID (*considering this owlishly*). Bed ? Yes, maybe you're right. (*He gets to his feet.*) I am not at all well —in very delicate condition—we are praying for a boy. Am I right, Nat ? Nat, I kept telling you all day I was in delicate condition and yet you kept forcing demon chowder on me, although you knew full well—even if you were full—that there is a certain, peculiar oil in chowder that invariably—— (*They are again all laughing—Lily, hysterically.*)

74

MRS. MILLER. *Will* you get to bed, you idiot !

SID (*mutters graciously*). Immediately—if not sooner. (*He turns to pass behind Lily, then stops, staring down at her.*) But wait. There is still a duty I must perform. No day is complete without it. Lily, answer once and for all, will you marry me ?

LILY (*with an hysterical giggle*). No, I won't—never !

SID (*nodding his head*). Right ! And perhaps it's all for the best. For how could I forget the pre—precepts taught me at mother's dying knee. " Sidney," she said, " never marry a woman who drinks ! Lips that touch liquor shall never touch yours ! " (*Gazing at her mournfully.*) Too bad ! So fine a woman once—and now such a slave to rum ! (*Turning to Miller.*) What can we do to save her, Nat ? (*In a hoarse, confidential whisper.*) Better put her in institution where she'll be removed from temptation ! The mere smell of it seems to drive her frantic !

MRS. MILLER (*struggling with her laughter*). You leave Lily alone, and go to bed !

SID. Right ! (*He comes around behind Lily's chair and moves toward the entrance to the back parlour—then suddenly turns and says with a bow.*) Good night, ladies —and gents. We will meet—by and by ! (*He gives an imitation of a Salvation Army drum.*) Boom ! Boom ! Boom ! Come and be saved, Brothers ! (*He starts to sing the old Army hymn.*)

> " In the sweet
> By and by
> We will meet on that beautiful shore."

(*He turns and marches solemnly out through the back parlour, singing.*)

" Work and pray
    While you may.
    We will meet in the sky by and by."

(*Miller and his wife and the children are all roaring
    with laughter. Lily giggles hysterically.*)

MILLER (*subsiding at last*). Haw, haw. He's a case, if
ever there was one ! Darned if you can help laughing
at him—even when he's poking fun at you !

MRS. MILLER. Goodness, but he's a caution ! Oh,
my sides ache, I declare ! I was trying so hard not to
—but you can't help it, he's so silly ! But I suppose
we really shouldn't. It only encourages him. But, my
lands—— !

LILY (*suddenly gets up from her chair and stands rigidly,
her face working—jerkily*). That's just it—you shouldn't
—even I laughed—it does encourage—that's been his
downfall—everyone always laughing, everyone always
saying what a card he is, what a case, what a caution,
so funny—and he's gone on—and we're all responsible
—making it easy for him—we're all to blame—and all
we do is laugh !

MILLER (*worriedly*). Now, Lily, now, you mustn't
take on so. It isn't as serious as all that.

LILY (*bitterly*). Maybe—it is—to me. Or was—
once. (*Then contritely.*) I'm sorry, Nat. I'm sorry,
Essie. I didn't mean to—I'm not feeling myself to-
night. If you'll excuse me, I'll go in the front parlour
and lie down on the sofa awhile.

MRS. MILLER. Of course, Lily. You do whatever
you've a mind to.

(*Lily goes out.*)

MILLER (*frowning—a little shamefaced*). Hmm. I suppose she's right. Never knew Lily to come out with things that way before. Anything special happened, Essie ?

MRS. MILLER. Nothing I know—except he'd promised to take her to the fireworks.

MILLER. That's so. Well, supposing I take her. I don't want her to feel disappointed.

MRS. MILLER (*shaking her head*). Wild horses couldn't drag her there now.

MILLER. Hmm. I thought she'd got completely over her foolishness about him long ago.

MRS. MILLER. She never will.

MILLER. She'd better. He's got fired out of that Waterbury job—told me at the picnic after he'd got enough Dutch courage in him.

MRS. MILLER. Oh, dear ! Isn't he the fool !

MILLER. I knew something was wrong when he came home. Well, I'll find a place for him on my paper again, of course. He always was the best news-getter this town ever had. But I'll tell him he's got to stop his damn nonsense.

MRS. MILLER (*doubtfully*). Yes.

MILLER. Well, no use sitting here mourning over spilt milk.

> (*He gets up, and Richard, Mildred, Tommy and Mrs. Miller follow his example, the children quiet and a bit awed.*)

You kids go out in the yard and try to keep quiet for a while, so's your Uncle Sid'll get to sleep and your Aunt Lily can rest.

TOMMY (*mournfully*). Ain't we going to set off the sky rockets and Roman candles, Pa ?

MILLER. Later, Son, later. It isn't dark enough for them yet anyway.

MILDRED. Come on, Tommy. I'll see he keeps quiet, Pa.

MILLER. That's a good girl.

> (*Mildred and Tommy go out through the screen door. Richard remains standing, sunk in bitter, gloomy thoughts.*)

(*Miller glances at him—then irritably.*) Well, Melancholy Dane, what are you doing ?

RICHARD (*darkly*). I'm going out—for a while. (*Then suddenly.*) Do you know what I think ? It's Aunt Lily's fault, Uncle Sid's going to ruin. It's all because he loves her, and she keeps him dangling after her, and eggs him on and ruins his life—like all women love to ruin men's lives ! I don't blame him for drinking himself to death ! What does he care if he dies, after the way she's treated him ! I'd do the same thing myself if I were in his boots !

MRS. MILLER (*indignantly*). Richard ! You stop that talk !

RICHARD (*quotes bitterly*).

" Drink ! for you know not whence you come nor why.
Drink ! for you know not why you go nor where ! "

MILLER (*losing his temper—harshly*). Listen here, young man ! I've had about all I can stand of your nonsense for one day ! You're growing a lot too big for your size, seems to me ! You keep that damn fool talk to yourself, you hear me—or you're going to regret it ! Mind, now ! (*He strides angrily away through the back parlour.*)

MRS. MILLER (*still indignant*). Richard, I'm ashamed of you, that's what I am.

> (*She follows her husband. Richard stands for a second, bitter, humiliated, wronged, even his father turned enemy, his face growing more and more rebellious. Then he forces a scornful smile to his lips.*)

RICHARD. Aw, what the hell do I care ? I'll show them ! (*He turns and goes out the screen door.*)

CURTAIN

ACT THREE

SCENE. *The back room of a bar in a small hotel—a small, dingy room, dimly lighted by two fly-specked globes in a fly-specked gilt chandelier suspended from the middle of the ceiling. At left, front, is the swinging door leading to the bar. At rear of door, against the wall, is a nickel-in-the-slot player-piano. In the rear wall, right, is a door leading to the " Family Entrance " and the stairway to the upstairs rooms. In the middle of the right wall is a window with closed shutters. Three tables with stained tops, four chairs around each table, are placed at centre, front, at right, toward rear, and at rear, centre. A brass cuspidor is on the floor by each table. The floor is unswept, littered with cigarette and cigar-butts. The hideous saffron-coloured wallpaper is blotched and spotted.*

It is about 10 *o'clock the same night. Richard and Belle are discovered sitting at the table at centre, Belle at left of it, Richard in the next chair at the middle of table, rear, facing front.*

Belle is twenty, a rather pretty peroxide blonde, a typical college " tart " of the period, and of the cheaper variety, dressed with tawdry flashiness. But she is a fairly recent recruit to the ranks, and is still a bit remorseful behind her make-up and defiantly careless manner.

Belle has an empty gin-rickey glass before her,

Richard a half-empty glass of beer. He looks horribly timid, embarrassed and guilty, but at the same time thrilled and proud of at last mingling with the pace that kills.

The player-piano is grinding out " Bedelia." The Bartender, a stocky young Irishman with a foxily cunning, stupid face and a cynically wise grin, stands just inside the bar entrance, watching them over the swinging door.

BELLE (*with an impatient glance at her escort—rattling the ice in her empty glass*). Drink up your beer, why don't you ? It's getting flat.

RICHARD (*embarrassedly*). I let it get that way on purpose. I like it better when it's flat.

> (*But he hastily gulps down the rest of his glass, as if it were some nasty-tasting medicine. The Bartender chuckles audibly. Belle glances at him.*)

BELLE (*nodding at the player-piano scornfully*). Say, George, is " Bedelia " the latest to hit this hick burg ? Well, it's only a couple of years old ! You'll catch up in time ! Why don't you get a new roll for that old box ?

BARTENDER (*with a grin*). Complain to the boss, not me. We're not used to having Candy Kiddoes like you around—or maybe we'd get up to date.

BELLE (*with a professionally arch grin at him*). Don't kid me, please. I can't bear it. (*Then she sings to the music from the piano, her eyes now on Richard.*) " Bedelia, I'd like to feel yer." (*The Bartender laughs. She smirks at Richard.*) Ever hear those words to it, Kid ?

RICHARD (*who has heard them but is shocked at hearing a girl say them—putting on a blasé air*). Sure, lots of times. That's old.

BELLE (*edging her chair closer and putting a hand over one of his*). Then why don't you act as if you knew what they were all about ?

RICHARD (*terribly flustered*). Sure, I've heard that old parody lots of times. What do you think I am ?

BELLE. I don't know, Kid. Honest to God, you've got me guessing.

BARTENDER (*with a mocking chuckle*). He's a hot sport, can't you tell it ? I never seen such a spender. My head's dizzy bringing you in drinks !

BELLE (*laughs irritably—to Richard*). Don't let him kid you. You show him. Loosen up and buy another drink, what say ?

RICHARD (*humiliated—manfully*). Sure. Excuse me. I was thinking of something else. Have anything you like. (*He turns to the Bartender who has entered from the bar.*) See what the lady will have—and have one on me yourself.

BARTENDER (*coming to the table—with a wink at Belle*). That's talking ! Didn't I say you were a sport ? I'll take a cigar on you. (*To Belle.*) What's yours, Kiddo —the same ?

BELLE. Yes. And forget the house rules this time and remember a rickey is supposed to have gin in it.

BARTENDER (*grinning*). I'll try to—seeing it's you. (*Then to Richard.*) What's yours—another beer ?

RICHARD (*shyly*). A small one, please. I'm not thirsty.

BELLE (*calculatedly taunting*). Say, honest, are things

that slow up at Harvard ? If they had you down at New Haven, they'd put you in a kindergarten ! Don' be such a dead one ! Filling up on beer will only make you sleepy. Have a man's drink !

RICHARD (*shamefacedly*). All right. I was going to. Bring me a sloe-gin fizz.

BELLE (*to Bartender*). And make it a real one.

BARTENDER (*with a wink*). I get you. Something that'll warm him up, eh ? (*He goes into the bar, chuckling.*)

BELLE (*looks around the room—irritably*). Christ, what a dump ! (*Richard is startled and shocked by this curse and looks down at the table.*) If this isn't the deadest burg I ever struck ! Bet they take the side-walks in after nine o'clock ! (*Then turning on him.*) Say, honestly, Kid, does your mother know you're out ?

RICHARD (*defensively*). Aw, cut it out, why don't you —trying to kid me !

BELLE (*glances at him—then resolves on a new tack—patting his hand*). All right. I didn't mean to, Dearie. Please don't get sore at me.

RICHARD. I'm not sore.

BELLE (*seductively*). You see, it's this way with me. I think you're one of the sweetest kids I've ever met— and I could like you such a lot if you'd give me half a chance—instead of acting so cold and indifferent.

RICHARD. I'm not cold and indifferent. (*Then solemnly tragic.*) It's only that I've got—a weight on my mind.

BELLE (*impatiently*). Well, get it off your mind and give something else a chance to work.

(The Bartender comes in, bringing the drinks.)

BARTENDER *(setting them down—with a wink at Belle)*. This'll warm him for you.   Forty cents, that is—with the cigar.

RICHARD *(pulls out his roll and hands a dollar bill over—with exaggerated carelessness)*.   Keep the change.

> *(Belle emits a gasp and seems about to protest, then thinks better of it. The Bartender cannot believe his luck for a moment—then pockets the bill hastily, as if afraid Richard will change his mind.)*

BARTENDER *(respect in his voice)*.   Thank you, sir.

RICHARD *(grandly)*.   Don't mention it.

BARTENDER.   I hope you like the drink.   I took special pains with it.   *(The voice of the Salesman, who has just come in the bar, calls " Hey !   Anybody here ? " and a coin is rapped on the bar.)*   I'm coming.   *(The Bartender goes out.)*

BELLE *(remonstrating gently, a new appreciation for her escort's possibilities in her voice)*.   You shouldn't be so generous, Dearie.   Gets him in bad habits.   A dime would have been plenty.

RICHARD.   Ah, that's all right.   I'm no tightwad.

BELLE.   That's the talk I like to hear.   *(With a quick look toward the bar, she stealthily pulls up her dress—to Richard's shocked fascination—and takes a package of cheap cigarettes from her stocking.)*   Keep an eye out for that bartender, Kid, and tell me if you see him coming. Girls are only allowed to smoke upstairs in the rooms, he said.

RICHARD (*embarrassedly*). All right. I'll watch.

BELLE (*having lighted her cigarette and inhaled deeply, holds the package out to him*). Have a Sweet ? You smoke, don't you ?

RICHARD (*taking one*). Sure ! I've been smoking for the last two years—on the sly. But next year I'll be allowed—that is, pipes and cigars. (*He lights his cigarette with elaborate nonchalance, puffs, but does not inhale—then, watching her, with shocked concern.*) Say, you oughtn't to inhale like that ! Smoking's awful bad for girls, any-way, even if they don't——

BELLE (*cynically amused*). Afraid it will stunt my growth ? Gee, Kid, you are a scream ! You'll grow up to be a minister yet ! (*Richard looks shamefaced. She scans him impatiently—then holds up her drink.*) Well, here's how ! Bottoms up, now ! Show me you really know how to drink. It'll take that load off your mind.

(*Richard follows her example, and they both drink the whole contents of their glasses before setting them down.*)

There ! That's something like ! Feel better ?

RICHARD (*proud of himself—with a shy smile*). You bet.

BELLE. Well, you'll feel still better in a minute—and then maybe you won't be so distant and unfriendly, eh ?

RICHARD. I'm not.

BELLE. Yes, you are. I think you just don't like me.

RICHARD (*more manfully*). I do too like you.

BELLE. How much ? A lot ?

RICHARD. Yes, a lot.

85

BELLE. Show me how much! (*Then as he fidgets embarrassedly.*) Want me to come sit on your lap?

RICHARD. Yes—I—— (*She comes and sits on his lap. He looks desperately uncomfortable, but the gin is rising to his head and he feels proud of himself and devilish, too.*)

BELLE. Why don't you put your arm around me? (*He does so awkwardly.*) No, not that dead way. Hold me tight. You needn't be afraid of hurting me. I like to be held tight, don't you?

RICHARD. Sure I do.

BELLE. 'Specially when it's by a nice handsome kid like you. (*Ruffling his hair.*) Gee, you've got pretty hair; do you know it? Honest, I'm awfully strong for you! Why can't you be about me? I'm not so awfully ugly, am I?

RICHARD. No, you're—you're pretty.

BELLE. You don't say it as if you meant it.

RICHARD. I do mean it—honest.

BELLE. Then why don't you kiss me? (*She bends down her lips toward his. He hesitates, then kisses her and at once shrinks back.*) Call that kissing? Here. (*She holds his head and fastens her lips on his and holds them there. He starts and struggles. She laughs.*) What's the matter, Honey Boy? Haven't you ever kissed like that before?

RICHARD. Sure. Lots of times.

BELLE. Then why did you jump as if I'd bitten you? (*Squirming around on his lap.*) Gee, I'm getting just crazy about you! What shall we do about it, eh? Tell me.

RICHARD. I—don't know. (*Then boldly.*) I—I'm crazy about you, too.

BELLE (*kissing him again*). Just think of the wonderful time Edith and your friend, Wint, are having upstairs —while we sit down here like two dead ones. A room only costs two dollars. And, seeing I like you so much, I'd only take five dollars—from you. I'd do it for nothing—for you—only I've got to live and I owe my room rent in New Haven—and you know how it is. I get ten dollars from everyone else. Honest ! (*She kisses him again, then gets up from his lap—briskly.*) Come on. Go out and tell the bartender you want a room. And hurry. Honest, I'm so strong for you I can hardly wait to get you upstairs !

RICHARD (*starts automatically for the door to the bar—then hesitates, a great struggle going on in his mind—timidity, disgust at the money element, shocked modesty, and the guilty thought of Muriel, fighting it out with the growing tipsiness that makes him want to be a hell of a fellow and go in for all forbidden fruit, and makes this tart a romantic, evil vampire in his eyes. Finally, he stops and mutters in confusion*). I can't.

BELLE. What, are you too bashful to ask for a room ? Let me do it, then.

(*She starts for the door.*)

RICHARD (*desperately*). No—I don't want you to—I don't want to.

BELLE (*surveying him, anger coming into her eyes*). Well, if you aren't the lousiest cheap skate !

RICHARD. I'm not a cheap skate !

BELLE. Keep me around here all night fooling with you when I might be out with some real live one—if there is such a thing in this burg !—and now you quit on me ! Don't be such a piker ! You've got five dollars ! I seen it when you paid for the drinks, so don't hand me any lies !

RICHARD. I—— Who said I hadn't ? And I'm not a piker. If you need the five dollars so bad—for your room rent—you can have it without—I mean, I'll be glad to give—— (*He has been fumbling in his pocket and pulls out his nine-dollar roll and holds out the five to her.*)

BELLE (*hardly able to believe her eyes, almost snatches it from his hand—then laughs and immediately becomes sentimentally grateful*). Thanks, Kid. Gee—oh, thanks—— Gee, forgive me for losing my temper and bawling you out, will you ? Gee, you're a regular peach ! You're the nicest kid I've ever met ! (*She kisses him and he grins proudly, a hero to himself now on many counts.*) Gee, you're a peach ! Thanks, again !

RICHARD (*grandly—and quite tipsily*). It's—nothing—only too glad. (*Then boldly.*) Here—give me another kiss, and that'll pay me back.

BELLE (*kissing him*). I'll give you a thousand, if you want 'em. Come on, let's sit down, and we'll have another drink—and this time I'll blow you just to show my appreciation. (*She calls.*) Hey, George ! Bring us another round—the same !

RICHARD (*a remnant of caution coming to him*). I don't know as I ought to——

BELLE. Oh, another won't hurt you. And I want to blow you, see.

(*They sit down in their former places.*)

RICHARD (*boldly draws his chair closer and puts an arm around her—tipsily*). I like you a lot—now I'm getting to know you. You're a darned nice girl.

BELLE. Nice is good ! Tell me another ! Well, if I'm so nice, why didn't you want to take me upstairs ? That's what I don't get.

RICHARD (*lying boldly*). I did want to—only I—— (*Then he adds solemnly.*) I've sworn off.

(*The Bartender enters with the drinks.*)

BARTENDER (*setting them on the table*). Here's your pleasure. (*Then regarding Richard's arm about her waist.*) Ho-ho, we're coming on, I see.

(*Richard grins at him muzzily.*)

BELLE (*digs into her stocking and gives him a dollar*). Here. This is mine. (*He gives her change and she tips him a dime, and he goes out. She puts the five Richard had given her in her stocking and picks up her glass.*) Here's how—and thanks again. (*She sips.*)

RICHARD (*boisterously*). Bottoms up ! Bottoms up ! (*He drinks all of his down and sighs with exaggerated satisfaction.*) Gee, that's good stuff, all right. (*Hugging her.*) Give me another kiss, Belle.

BELLE (*kisses him*). What did you mean a minute ago when you said you'd sworn off ?

RICHARD (*solemnly*). I took an oath I'd be faithful.

BELLE (*cynically*). Till death do us part, eh ? Who's the girl ?

RICHARD (*shortly*). Never mind.

BELLE (*bristling*).   I'm not good enough to talk about her, I suppose ?

RICHARD.   I didn't—mean that.   You're all right. (*Then with tipsy gravity.*)   Only you oughtn't to lead this kind of life.   It isn't right—for a nice girl like you. Why don't you reform ?

BELLE (*sharply*).   Nix on that line of talk !   Can it, you hear !   You can do a lot with me for five dollars —but you can't reform me, see.   Mind your own business, Kid, and don't butt in where you're not wanted !

RICHARD.   I—I didn't mean to hurt your feelings.

BELLE.   I know you didn't mean.   You're only like a lot of people who mean well, to hear them tell it.   (*Changing the subject.*)   So you're faithful to your one love, eh ? (*With an ugly sneer.*)   And how about her ?   Bet you she's out with a guy under some bush this minute, giving him all he wants.   Don't be a sucker, Kid !   Even the little flies do it !

RICHARD (*starting up in his chair—angrily*).   Don't you say that.   Don't you dare !

BELLE (*unimpressed—with a cynical shrug of her shoulders*). All right.   Have it your own way and be a sucker !   It cuts no ice with me.

RICHARD.   You don't know her or——

BELLE.   And don't want to.   Shut up about her, can't you ?

> (*She stares before her bitterly.   Richard subsides into scowling gloom.   He is becoming perceptibly more intoxicated with each moment now. The Bartender and the Salesman appear just*

inside the swinging door. The Bartender nods toward Belle, giving the Salesman a drink. The Salesman grins and comes into the room, carrying his highball in his hand. He is a stout, jowly-faced man in his late thirties, dressed with cheap nattiness, with the professional breeziness and jocular, kid-'em-along manner of his kind. Belle looks up as he enters and he and she exchange a glance of complete recognition. She knows his type by heart and he knows hers.)

SALESMAN (*passes by her to the table at right—grinning genially*). Good evening.

BELLE. Good evening.

SALESMAN (*sitting down*). Hope I'm not butting in on your party—but my dogs were giving out standing at that bar.

BELLE. All right with me. (*Giving Richard a rather contemptuous look.*) I've got no party on.

SALESMAN. That sounds hopeful.

RICHARD (*suddenly recites sentimentally*).

" But I wouldn't do such, 'cause I loved her too much,
But I learned about women from her."

(*Turns to scowl at the Salesman—then to Belle.*) Let's have 'nother drink !

BELLE. You've had enough.

    (*Richard subsides, muttering to himself.*)

SALESMAN. What is it—a child poet or a child actor ?

BELLE. Don't know. Got me guessing.

SALESMAN. Well, if you could shake the cradle-robbing act, maybe we could do a little business.

BELLE. That's easy. I just pull my freight. (*She shakes Richard by the arm.*) Listen, Kid. Here's an old friend of mine, Mr. Smith of New Haven, just come in. I'm going over and sit at his table for a while, see. And you better go home.

RICHARD (*blinking at her and scowling*). I'm never going home ! I'll show them !

BELLE. Have it your own way—only let me up.

> (*She takes his arm from around her and goes to sit by the Salesman. Richard stares after her offendedly.*)

RICHARD. Go on. What do I care what you do ? (*He recites scornfully.*) " For a woman's only a woman, but a good cigar's a smoke."

SALESMAN (*as Belle sits beside him*). Well, what kind of beer will you have, Sister ?

BELLE. Mine's a gin rickey.

SALESMAN. You've got extravagant tastes, I'm sorry to see.

RICHARD (*begins to recite sepulchrally*).

> " Yet each man kills the thing he loves,
> By each let this be heard."

SALESMAN (*grinning*). Say, this is rich ! (*He calls encouragement.*) That's swell dope, young feller. Give us some more.

RICHARD (*ignoring him—goes on more rhetorically*).

" Some do it with a bitter look,
Some with a flattering word,
The coward does it with a kiss,
The brave man with a sword ! "

(*He stares at Belle gloomily and mutters tragically.*)   I did it
with a kiss !   I'm a coward.

SALESMAN.   That's the old stuff, Kid.   You've got
something on the ball, all right, all right !   Give us
another—right over the old pan, now !

BELLE (*with a laugh*).   Get the hook !

RICHARD (*glowering at her—tragically*).

" ' Oho,' they cried, ' the world is wide,
But fettered limbs go lame !
And once, or twice, to throw the dice
Is a gentlemanly game,
But he does not win who plays with Sin
In the secret House of Shame ! ' "

BELLE (*angrily*).   Aw, can it !   Give us a rest from
that bunk !

SALESMAN (*mockingly*).   This gal of yours don't appreciate poetry.   She's a lowbrow.   But I'm the kid that
eats it up.   My middle name is Kelly and Sheets !   Give
us some more of the same !   Do you know " The Lobster and the Wise Guy " ?   (*Turns to Belle seriously.*)
No kidding, that's a peacherino.   I heard a guy recite
it at Poli's.   Maybe this nut knows it.   Do you, Kid ?
(*But Richard only glowers at him gloomily without answering.*)

BELLE (*surveying Richard contemptuously*).   He's copped
a fine skinful—and gee, he's hardly had anything.

RICHARD (*suddenly—with a dire emphasis*).   " And

then—at ten o'clock—Eilert Lovborg wiil come—with vine leaves in his hair ! "

BELLE.   And bats in his belfry, if he's you !

RICHARD (*regards her bitterly—then starts to his feet bellicosely—to the Salesman*).   I don't believe you ever knew her in New Haven at all !   You just picked her up now !   You leave her alone, you hear !   You won't do anything to her—not while I'm here to protect her !

BELLE (*laughing*).   Oh, my God !   Listen to it !

SALESMAN.   Ssshh !   This is a scream !   Wait !   (*He addresses Richard in tones of exaggerated melodrama.*) Curse you, Jack Dalton, if I won't unhand her, what then ?

RICHARD (*threateningly*).   I'll give you a good punch in the snoot, that's what !   (*He moves toward their table.*)

SALESMAN (*with mock terror—screams in falsetto*).   Help! Help !

(*The Bartender comes in irritably.*)

BARTENDER.   Hey.   Cut out the noise.   What the hell's up with you ?

RICHARD (*tipsily*).   He's too—damn fresh !

SALESMAN (*with a wink*).   He's going to murder me ! (*Then gets a bright idea for eliminating Richard—seriously to the Bartender.*)   It's none of my business, Brother, but if I were in your boots I'd give this young souse the gate.   He's under age ; any fool can see that.

BARTENDER (*guiltily*).   He told me he was over eighteen.

SALESMAN.   Yes, and I tell you I'm the Pope—but you

don't have to believe me. If you're not looking for trouble, I'd advise you to get him started for some other gin mill and let them do the lying, if anything comes up.

BARTENDER. Hmm. (*He turns to Richard angrily and gives him a push.*) Come on, now. On your way ! You'll start no trouble in here ! Beat it now !

RICHARD. I will not beat it !

BARTENDER. Oho, won't you ? (*He gives him another push that almost sends him sprawling.*)

BELLE (*callously*). Give him the bum's rush ! I'm sick of his bull !

(*Richard turns furiously and tries to punch the Bartender.*)

BARTENDER (*avoids the punch*). Oho, you would, would you ! (*He grabs Richard by the back of the neck and the seat of the pants and marches him ignominiously toward the swinging door.*)

RICHARD. Leggo of me, you dirty coward !

BARTENDER. Quiet now—or I'll pin a Mary Ann on your jaw that'll quiet you ! (*He rushes him through the screen door and a moment later the outer doors are heard swinging back and forth.*)

SALESMAN (*with a chuckle*). Hand it to me, Kid. How was that for a slick way of getting rid of him ?

BELLE (*suddenly sentimental*). Poor kid. I hope he makes home all right. I liked him—before he got soused.

SALESMAN. Who is he ?

95

BELLE. The boy who's upstairs with my friend told me, but I didn't pay much attention. Name's Miller. His old man runs a paper in this one-horse burg, I think he said.

SALESMAN (*with a whistle*). Phew ! He must be Nat Miller's kid, then.

BARTENDER (*coming back from the bar*). Well, he's on his way—with a good boot in the tail to help him !

SALESMAN (*with a malicious chuckle*). Yes ? Well maybe that boot will cost you a job, Brother. Know Nat Miller who runs the " Globe " ? That's his kid.

BARTENDER (*his face falling*). The hell he is ! Who said so ?

SALESMAN. This baby doll. (*Getting up.*) Say, I'll go keep cases on him—see he gets on the trolley all right, anyway. Nat Miller's a good scout. (*He hurries out.*)

BARTENDER (*viciously*). God damn the luck ! If he ever finds out I served his kid, he'll run me out of town. (*He turns on Belle furiously.*) Why didn't you put me wise, you lousy tramp, you !

BELLE. Hey ! I don't stand for that kind of talk —not from no hick beer-squirter like you, see !

BARTENDER (*furiously*). You don't, don't you ! Who was it but you told me to hand him dynamite in that fizz ? (*He gives her chair a push that almost throws her to the floor.*) Beat it, you—and beat it quick—or I'll call Sullivan from the corner and have you run in for street-walking ! (*He gives her a push that lands her against the family-entrance door.*) Get the hell out of here—and no long waits !

BELLE (*opens the door and goes out—turns and calls back viciously*). I'll fix you for this, you thick Mick, if I have to go to jail for it. (*She goes out and slams the door.*)

BARTENDER (*looks after her worriedly for a second—then shrugs his shoulders*). That's only her bull. (*Then with a sigh as he returns to the bar.*) Them lousy tramps is always getting this dump in Dutch !

CURTAIN

SCENE TWO

SCENE. *Same as Act One—Sitting-room of the Miller home—about* 11 *o'clock the same night.*

Miller is sitting in his favourite rocking-chair at left of table, front. He has discarded collar and tie, coat and shoes, and wears an old, worn, brown dressing-gown and disreputable-looking carpet slippers. He has his reading specs on and is running over items in a newspaper. But his mind is plainly preoccupied and worried, and he is not paying much attention to what he reads.

Mrs. Miller sits by the table at right, front. She also has on her specs. A sewing-basket is on her lap and she is trying hard to keep her attention fixed on the doily she is doing. But, as in the case of her husband, but much more apparently, her mind is preoccupied, and she is obviously on tenterhooks of nervous uneasiness.

Lily is sitting in the armchair by the table at rear, facing right. She is pretending to read a novel, but her attention wanders, too, and her expression is sad, although now it has lost all its bitterness and become submissive and resigned again.

97

Mildred sits at the desk at right, front, writing two words over and over again, stopping each time to survey the result critically, biting her tongue, intensely concentrated on her work.

Tommy sits on the sofa at left, front. He has had a hard day and is terribly sleepy but will not acknowledge it. His eyes blink shut on him, his head begins to nod, but he isn't giving up, and every time he senses any of the family glancing in his direction, he goads himself into a bright-eyed wakefulness.

MILDRED (*finally surveys the two words she has been writing and is satisfied with them*). There. (*She takes the paper over to her mother.*) Look, Ma. I've been practising a new way of writing my name. Don't look at the others, only the last one. Don't you think it's the real goods ?

MRS. MILLER (*pulled out of her preoccupation*). Don't talk that horrible slang. It's bad enough for boys, but for a young girl supposed to have manners—my goodness, when I was your age, if my mother'd ever heard me——

MILDRED. Well, don't you think it's nice, then ?

MRS. MILLER (*sinks back into preoccupation—scanning the paper—vaguely*). Yes, very nice, Mildred—very nice, indeed. (*Hands the paper back mechanically.*)

MILDRED (*is a little piqued, but smiles*). Absent-minded ! I don't believe you even saw it.

(*She passes around the table to show her Aunt Lily. Miller gives an uneasy glance at his wife and then, as if afraid of meeting her eye, looks quickly back at his paper again.*)

MRS. MILLER (*staring before her—sighs worriedly*). Oh, I do wish Richard would come home !

MILLER. There now, Essie. He'll be in any minute now. Don't you worry about him.

MRS. MILLER. But I do worry about him !

LILY (*surveying Mildred's handiwork—smiling*). This is fine, Mildred. Your penmanship is improving wonderfully. But don't you think that maybe you've got a little too many flourishes ?

MILDRED (*disappointedly*). But, Aunt Lily, that's just what I was practising hardest on.

MRS. MILLER (*with another sigh*). What time is it now, Nat ?

MILLER (*adopting a joking tone*). I'm going to buy a clock for in here. You have me reaching for my watch every couple of minutes. (*He has pulled his watch out of his vest pocket—with forced carelessness.*) Only a little past ten.

MRS. MILLER. Why, you said it was that an hour ago ! Nat Miller, you're telling me a fib, so's not to worry me. You let me see that watch !

MILLER (*guiltily*). Well, it's quarter to eleven—but that's not so late—when you remember it's Fourth of July.

MRS. MILLER. If you don't stop talking Fourth of July——— ! To hear you go on, you'd think that was an excuse for anything from murder to picking pockets !

MILDRED (*has brought her paper around to her father and now shoves it under his nose*). Look, Pa.

MILLER (*seizes on this interruption with relief*). Let's see. Hmm. Seems to me you've been inventing a new signature every week lately. What are you in training for—writing cheques ? You must be planning to catch a rich husband.

MILDRED (*with an a rchtoss of her head*). No wedding bells for me ! But how do you like it, Pa ?

MILLER. It's overpowering—no other word for it, overpowering ! You could put it on the Declaration of Independence and not feel ashamed.

MRS. MILLER (*desolately, almost on the verge of tears*). It's all right for you to laugh and joke with Mildred ! I'm the only one in this house seems to care—— (*Her lips tremble.*)

MILDRED (*a bit disgustedly*). Ah, Ma, Dick only sneaked off to the fireworks at the beach, you wait and see.

MRS. MILLER. Those fireworks were over long ago. If he had, he'd be home.

LILY (*soothingly*). He probably couldn't get a seat, the trolleys are so jammed, and he had to walk home.

MILLER (*seizing on this with relief*). Yes, I never thought of that, but I'll bet that's it.

MILDRED. Ah, don't let him worry you, Ma. He just wants to show off he's heart-broken about that silly Muriel—and get everyone fussing over him and wondering if he hasn't drowned himself or something.

MRS. MILLER (*snappily*). You be quiet ! The way you talk at times, I really believe you're that hard-hearted you haven't got a heart in you ! (*With an accusing glance at her husband.*) One thing I know, you don't get that from me !

(He meets her eye and avoids it guiltily. She sniffs and looks away from him around the room. Tommy, who is nodding and blinking, is afraid her eye is on him. He straightens alertly and speaks in a voice that, in spite of his effort, is dripping with drowsiness.)

TOMMY. Let me see what you wrote, Mid.

MILDRED *(cruelly mocking)*. You ? You're so sleepy you couldn't see it !

TOMMY *(valiantly)*. I am not sleepy !

MRS. MILLER *(has fixed her eye on him)*. My gracious, I was forgetting you were still up ! You run up to bed this minute ! It's hours past your bedtime !

TOMMY. But it's the Fourth of July. Ain't it, Pa ?

MRS. MILLER *(gives her husband an accusing stare)*. There ! You see what you've done ? You might know he'd copy your excuses ! *(Then sharply to Tommy.)* You heard what I said, Young Man !

TOMMY. Aw, Ma, can't I stay up a *little* longer ?

MRS. MILLER. I said, no ! You obey me and no more arguing about it !

TOMMY *(drags himself to his feet)*. Aw ! I should think I could stay up till Dick——

MILLER *(kindly but firmly)*. You heard your ma say no more arguing. When she says git, you better git.

(Tommy accepts his fate resignedly and starts around kissing them all good night.)

TOMMY *(kissing her)*. Good night, Aunt Lily.

LILY.   Good night, dear.   Sleep well.

TOMMY (*pecking at Mildred*).   Good night, you.

MILDRED.   Good night, you.

TOMMY (*kissing him*).   Good night, Pa.

MILLER.   Good night, Son.   Sleep tight.

TOMMY (*kissing her*).   Good night, Ma.

MRS. MILLER.   Good night.   Here !   You look fever-ish.   Let me feel of your head.   No, you're all right.   Hurry up, now.   And don't forget your prayers.

> (*Tommy goes slowly to the doorway—then turns sud-denly, the discovery of another excuse lighting up his face.*)

TOMMY.   Here's another thing, Ma.   When I was up to the water-closet last——

MRS. MILLER (*sharply*).   When you were *where* ?

TOMMY.   The bathroom.

MRS. MILLER.   That's better.

TOMMY.   Uncle Sid was snoring like a fog-horn—and he's right next to my room.   How can I ever get to sleep while he's—— (*He is overcome by a jaw-cracking yawn.*)

MRS. MILLER.   I guess you'd get to sleep all right if you were inside a fog-horn.   You run along now.

> (*Tommy gives up, grins sleepily, and moves off to bed. As soon as he is off her mind, all her former uneasiness comes back on Mrs. Miller tenfold. She sighs, moves restlessly, then finally asks:*)

What time is it now, Nat ?

MILLER. Now, Essie, I just told you a minute ago.

MRS. MILLER (*resentfully*). I don't see how you can take it so calm ! Here it's midnight, you might say, and our Richard still out, and we don't even know where he is.

MILDRED. I hear someone on the piazza. Bet that's him now, Ma.

MRS. MILLER (*her anxiety immediately turning to relieved anger*). You give him a good piece of your mind, Nat, you hear me ! You're too easy with him, that's the whole trouble ! The idea of him daring to stay out like this !

> (*The front door is heard being opened and shut, and someone whistling " Watlz Me Around Again, Willie."*)

MILDRED. No, that isn't Dick. It's Art.

MRS. MILLER (*her face falling*). Oh.

> (*A moment later Arthur enters through the front parlour, whistling softly, half under his breath, looking complacently pleased with himself.*)

MILLER (*surveys him over his glasses, not with enthusiasm —shortly*). So you're back, eh ? We thought it was Richard.

ARTHUR. Is he still out ? Where'd he go to ?

MILLER. That's just what we'd like to know. You didn't run into him anywhere, did you ?

ARTHUR. No. I've been at the Rands' ever since

dinner. (*He sits down in the armchair at left of table, rear.*) I suppose he sneaked off to the beach to watch the fireworks.

MILLER (*pretending an assurance he is far from feeling*). Of course. That's what we've been trying to tell your mother, but she insists on worrying her head off.

MRS. MILLER. But if he was going to the fireworks, why wouldn't he say so ? He knew we'd let him.

ARTHUR (*with calm wisdom*). That's easy, Ma. (*He grins superiorly.*) Didn't you hear him this morning showing off bawling out the Fourth like an anarchist ? He wouldn't want to reneg on that to you—but he'd want to see the old fireworks just the same. (*He adds complacently.*) I know. He's at the foolish age.

MILLER (*stares at Arthur with ill-concealed astonishment, then grins*). Well, Arthur, by gosh, you make me feel as if I owed you an apology when you talk horse sense like that. (*He turns to his wife, greatly relieved.*) Arthur's hit the nail right on the head, I think, Essie. That was what I couldn't figure out—why he—but now it's clear as day.

MRS. MILLER (*with a sigh*). Well, I hope you're right. But I wish he was home.

ARTHUR (*takes out his pipe and fills and lights it with solemn gravity*). He oughtn't to be allowed out this late at his age. I wasn't, Fourth or no Fourth—if I remember.

MILLER (*a twinkle in his eyes*). Don't tax your memory trying to recall those ancient days of your youth.

(*Mildred laughs and Arthur looks sheepish. But he soon regains his aplomb.*)

ARTHUR (*importantly*).   We had a corking dinner at the Rands'.   We had sweetbreads on toast.

MRS. MILLER (*arising momentarily from her depression*). Just like the Rands to put on airs before you !   I never could see anything to sweetbreads.   Always taste like soap to me.   And no real nourishment to them.   I wouldn't have the pesky things on my table !

(*Arthur again feels sat upon.*)

MILDRED (*teasingly*).   Did you kiss Elsie good night ?

ARTHUR.   Stop trying to be so darn funny all the time !   You give me a pain in the ear !

MILDRED.   And that's where she gives me a pain, the stuck-up thing !—thinks she's the whole cheese !

MILLER (*irritably*).   And it's where your everlasting wrangling gives me a pain, you two !   Give us a rest !

(*There is silence for a moment.*)

MRS. MILLER (*sighs worriedly again*).   I do wish that boy would get home !

MILLER (*glances at her uneasily, peeks surreptitiously at his watch—then has an inspiration and turns to Arthur*). Arthur, what's this I hear about your having such a good singing voice ?   Rand was telling me he liked nothing better than to hear you sing—said you did every night you were up there.   Why don't you ever give us folks at home here a treat ?

ARTHUR (*pleased, but still nursing wounded dignity*).   I thought you'd only sit on me.

MRS. MILLER (*perking up—proudly*).   Arthur has a real

nice voice. He practises when you're not at home. I didn't know you cared for singing, Nat.

MILLER. Well, I do—nothing better—and when I was a boy I had a fine voice myself and folks used to say I'd ought—— (*Then abruptly, mindful of his painful experience with reminiscence at dinner, looking about him guiltily.*) Hmm. But don't hide your light under a bushel, Arthur. Why not give us a song or two now ? You can play for him, can't you, Mildred ?

MILDRED (*with a toss of her head*). I can play as well as Elsie Rand, at least !

ARTHUR (*ignoring her—clearing his throat importantly*). I've been singing a lot to-night. I don't know if my voice——

MILDRED (*forgetting her grudge, grabs her brother's hand and tugs at it*). Come on. Don't play modest. You know you're just dying to show off.

(*This puts Arthur off it at once. He snatches his hand away from her angrily.*)

ARTHUR. Let go of me, you ! (*Then with surly dignity.*) I don't feel like singing to-night, Pa. I will some other time.

MILLER. You let him alone, Mildred !

(*He winks at Arthur, indicating with his eyes and a nod of his head Mrs. Miller, who has again sunk into worried brooding. He makes it plain by this pantomime that he wants him to sing to distract his mother's mind.*)

ARTHUR (*puts aside his pipe and gets up promptly*). Oh— sure, I'll do the best I can. (*He follows Mildred into the front parlour, where he switches on the lights.*)

MILLER (*to his wife*). It won't keep Tommy awake. Nothing could. And Sid, he'd sleep through an earthquake. (*Then suddenly, looking through the front parlour —grumpily.*) Darn it, speak of the devil, here he comes. Well, he's had a good sleep and he'd ought to be sobered up. (*Lily gets up from her chair and looks around her huntedly, as if for a place to hide. Miller says soothingly:*) Lily, you just sit down and read your book and don't pay any attention to him.

> (*She sits down again and bends over her book tensely. From the front parlour comes the tinkling of a piano as Mildred runs over the scales. In the midst of this, Sid enters through the front parlour. All the effervescence of his jag has worn off and he is now suffering from a bad case of hangover—nervous, sick, a prey to gloomy remorse and bitter feelings of self-loathing and self-pity. His eyes are bloodshot and puffed, his face bloated, the fringe of hair around his baldness tousled and tufty. He sidles into the room guiltily, his eyes shifting about, avoiding looking at anyone.*)

SID (*forcing a sickly, twitching smile*). Hello.

MILLER (*considerately casual*). Hello, Sid. Had a good nap ?

> (*Then, as Sid swallows hard and is about to break into further speech, Mildred's voice comes from the front parlour, " I haven't played that in ever so long, but I ll try," and she starts an accompaniment. Miller motions Sid to be quiet.*)

Ssshh ! Arthur's going to sing for us.

(*Sid flattens himself against the edge of the bookcase at centre, rear, miserably self-conscious and ill at ease there but nervously afraid to move anywhere else. Arthur begins to sing. He has a fairly decent voice but his method is untrained sentimentality to a dripping degree. He sings that old sentimental favourite, " Then You'll Remember Me." The effect on his audience is instant. Miller gazes before him with a ruminating melancholy, his face seeming to become gently sorrowful and old. Mrs. Miller stares before her, her expression becoming more and more doleful. Lily forgets to pretend to read her book but looks over it, her face growing tragically sad. As for Sid, he is moved to his remorseful, guilt-stricken depths. His mouth pulls down at the corners and he seems about to cry. The song comes to an end. Miller starts, then claps his hands enthusiastically and calls :*)

Well done, Arthur—well done ! Why, you've got a splendid voice ! Give us some more ! You liked that, didn't you, Essie ?

MRS. MILLER (*dolefully*). Yes—but it's sad—terrible sad.

SID (*after swallowing hard, suddenly blurts out*). Nat and Essie—and Lily—I—I want to apologize—for coming home—the way I did—there's no excuse—but I didn't mean——

MILLER (*sympathetically*). Of course, Sid. It's all forgotten.

MRS. MILLER (*rousing herself—affectionately pitying*).

Don't be a goose, Sid.   We know how it is with picnics.
You forget it.

> (*His face lights up a bit but his gaze shifts to Lily
> with a mute appeal, hoping for a word from
> her which is not forthcoming.   Her eyes are
> fixed on her book, her body tense and rigid.*)

SID (*finally blurts out desperately*).   Lily—I'm sorry—
about the fireworks.   Can you—forgive me ?

> (*But Lily remains implacably silent.   A stricken
> look comes over Sid's face.   In the front par-
> lour Mildred is heard saying* " But I only know
> the chorus "—*and she starts another accom-
> paniment.*)

MILLER (*comes to Sid's rescue*).   Ssshh !   We're going
to have another song.   Sit down, Sid.

> (*Sid, hanging his head, flees to the farthest corner,
> left, front, and sits at the end of the sofa, fac-
> ing front, hunched up, elbows on knees, face
> in hands, his round eyes childishly wounded
> and woebegone.   Arthur sings the popular
> " Dearie," playing up its sentimental values
> for all he is worth.   The effect on his audience
> is that of the previous song, intensified—especi-
> ally upon Sid.   As he finishes, Miller again
> starts and applauds.*)

Mighty fine, Arthur !   You sang that darned well !
Didn't he, Essie ?

MRS. MILLER (*dolefully*).   Yes—but I wish he wouldn't
sing such sad songs.   (*Then, her lips trembling.*)
Richard's always whistling that.

MILLER (*hastily—calls*). Give us something cheery, next one, Arthur. You know, just for variety's sake.

SID (*suddenly turns toward Lily—his voice choked with tears—in a passion of self-denunciation*). You're right, Lily !—right not to forgive me !—I'm no good and never will be !—I'm a no-good drunken bum !—you shouldn't even wipe your feet on me !—I'm a dirty, rotten drunk !—no good to myself or anybody else !—if I had any guts I'd kill myself, and good riddance !—but I haven't !—I'm yellow, too !—a yellow, drunken bum !

> (*He hides his face in his hands and begins to sob like a sick little boy. This is too much for Lily. All her bitter hurt and steely resolve to ignore and punish him vanish in a flash, swamped by a pitying love for him. She runs and puts her arm around him—even kisses him tenderly and impulsively on his bald head, and soothes him as if he were a little boy. Mrs. Miller, almost equally moved, has half risen to go to her brother, too, but Miller winks and shakes his head vigorously and motions her to sit down.*)

LILY. There ! Don't cry, Sid ! I can't bear it ! Of course, I forgive you ! Haven't I always forgiven you ? I know you're not to blame—— So don't, Sid !

SID (*lifts a tearful, humbly grateful, pathetic face to her—but a face that the dawn of a cleansed conscience is already beginning to restore to its natural Puckish expression*). Do you really forgive me—— I know I don't deserve it —can you really—— ?

LILY (*gently*). I told you I did, Sid—and I do.

SID (*kisses her hand humbly, like a big puppy licking it*). Thanks, Lily. I can't tell you——

> (*In the front parlour, Arthur begins to sing rollickingly " Waiting at the Church," and after the first line or two Mildred joins in. Sid's face lights up with appreciation and, automatically, he begins to tap one foot in time, still holding fast to Lily's hand. When they come to " sent around a note, this is what she wrote," he can no longer resist, but joins in a shaky bawl.*)

" Can't get away to marry you to-day, My wife won't let me ! "

> (*As the song finishes, the two in the other room laugh. Miller and Sid laugh. Lily smiles at Sid's laughter. Only Mrs. Miller remains dolefully preoccupied, as if she hadn't heard.*)

MILLER. That's fine, Arthur and Mildred. That's darned good.

SID (*turning to Lily enthusiastically*). You ought to hear Vesta Victoria sing that ! Gosh, she's great ! I heard her at Hammerstein's Victoria—you remember, that trip I made to New York.

LILY (*her face suddenly tired and sad again—for her memory of certain aspects of that trip is the opposite from what he would like her to recall at this moment—gently disengaging her hand from his—with a hopeless sigh*). Yes, I remember, Sid.

> (*He is overcome momentarily by guilty confusion. She goes quietly and sits down in her chair again. In the front parlour, from now on, Mildred keeps starting to run over popular tunes but always gets stuck and turns to another.*)

111

MRS. MILLER (*suddenly*).   What time is it now, Nat ?
(*Then without giving him a chance to answer.*)   Oh, I'm
getting worried something dreadful, Nat !   You don't
know what might have happened to Richard !   You read
in the papers every day about boys getting run over by
automobiles.

LILY.   Oh, don't say that, Essie !

MILLER (*sharply, to conceal his own reawakened apprehension*).   Don't get to imagining things, now !

MRS. MILLER.   Well, why couldn't it happen, with
everyone that owns one out to-night, and lots of those
driving, drunk ?   Or he might have gone down to the
beach dock and fallen overboard !   (*On the verge of
hysteria.*)   Oh, I know something dreadful's happened !
And you can sit there listening to songs and laughing as
if——   Why don't you do something ?   Why don't
you go out and find him ?   (*She bursts into tears.*)

LILY (*comes to her quickly and puts her arm around her*).
Essie, you mustn't worry so !   You'll make yourself
sick !   Richard's all right.   I've got a feeling in my
bones he's all right.

MILDRED (*comes hurrying in from the front parlour*).
What's the trouble ?   (*Arthur appears in the doorway
beside her.   She goes to her mother and also puts an arm
around her.*)   Ah, don't cry, Ma !   Dick'll turn up in
a minute or two, wait and see !

ARTHUR.   Sure, he will !

MILLER (*has gotten to his feet, frowning—soberly*).   I was
going out to look—if he wasn't back by twelve sharp.
That'd be the time it'd take him to walk from the beach
if he left after the last car.   But I'll go now, if it'll ease

your mind. I'll take the auto and drive out the beach road—and likely pick him up on the way. (*He has taken his collar and tie from where they hang from one corner of the bookcase at rear, centre, and is starting to put them on.*) You better come with me, Arthur.

ARTHUR. Sure thing, Pa. (*Suddenly he listens and says.*) Ssshh ! There's someone on the piazza now— coming around to this door, too. That must be him. No one else would——

MRS. MILLER. Oh, thank God, thank God !

MILLER (*with a sheepish smile*). Darn him ! I've a notion to give him hell for worrying us all like this.

> (*The screen door is pushed violently open and Richard lurches in and stands swaying a little, blinking his eyes in the light. His face is a pasty pallor, shining with perspiration, and his eyes are glassy. The knees of his trousers are dirty, one of them torn from the sprawl on the side-walk he had taken, following the Bartender's kick. They all gape at him, too paralysed for a moment to say anything.*)

MRS. MILLER. Oh God, what's happened to him ! He's gone crazy ! Richard !

SID (*the first to regain presence of mind—with a grin*). Crazy, nothing. He's only soused !

ARTHUR. He's drunk, that's what ! (*Then shocked and condemning.*) You've got your nerve ! You fresh kid ! We'll take that out of you when we get you down to Yale !

RICHARD (*with a wild gesture of defiance—maudlinly dramatic*).

"Yesterday this Day's Madness did prepare
To-morrow's Silence, Triumph, or Despair.
Drink ! for——"

MILLER (*his face grown stern and angry, takes a threatening step toward him*). Richard ! How dare—— !

MRS. MILLER (*hysterically*). Don't you strike him, Nat ! Don't you—— !

SID (*grabbing his arm*). Steady, Nat ! Keep your temper ! No good bawling him out now ! He don't know what he's doing !

MILLER (*controlling himself and looking a bit ashamed*). All right—you're right, Sid.

RICHARD (*drunkenly glorying in the sensation he is creating —recites with dramatic emphasis*). "And then—I will come—with vine leaves in my hair !" (*He laughs with a double-dyed sardonicism.*)

MRS. MILLER (*staring at him as if she couldn't believe her eyes*). Richard ! You're intoxicated !—you bad, wicked boy, you !

RICHARD (*forces a wicked leer to his lips and quotes with ponderous mockery*). "Fancy that, Hedda !" (*Then suddenly his whole expression changes, his pallor takes on a greenish, seasick tinge, his eyes seem to be turned inward uneasily—and, all pose gone, he calls to his mother appealingly, like a sick little boy.*) Ma ! I feel—rotten !

(*Mrs. Miller gives a cry and starts to go to him, but Sid steps in her way.*)

SID. You let me take care of him, Essie. I know this game backwards.

MILLER (*putting his arm around his wife*). Yes, you leave him to Sid.

SID (*his arm around Richard—leading him off through the front parlour*). Come on, Old Sport ! Upstairs we go ! Your old Uncle Sid'll fix you up. He's the kid that wrote the book !

MRS. MILLER (*staring after them—still aghast*). Oh, it's too terrible ! Imagine our Richard ! And did you hear him talking about some Hedda ? Oh, I know he's been with one of those bad women, I know he has—my Richard ! (*She hides her face on Miller's shoulder and sobs heart-brokenly.*)

MILLER (*a tired, harassed, deeply worried look on his face —soothing her*). Now, now, you mustn't get to imagining such things ! You mustn't, Essie ! (*Lily and Mildred and Arthur are standing about awkwardly with awed, shocked faces.*)

CURTAIN

ACT FOUR

SCENE ONE

SCENE. *The same—Sitting-room of the Miller house—
about 1 o'clock in the afternoon of the following day.*

*As the curtain rises, the family, with the exception of
Richard, are discovered coming in through the back
parlour from dinner in the dining-room. Miller and
his wife come first. His face is set in an expression
of frowning severity. Mrs. Miller's face is drawn and
worried. She has evidently had no rest yet from a
sleepless, tearful night. Sid is himself again, his
expression as innocent as if nothing had occurred the
previous day that remotely concerned him. And, outside of eyes that are bloodshot and nerves that are
shaky, he shows no after-effects except that he is terribly
sleepy. Lily is gently sad and depressed. Arthur is
self-consciously a virtuous young man against whom
nothing can be said. Mildred and Tommy are subdued,
covertly watching their father.*

*They file into the sitting-room in silence and then
stand around uncertainly, as if each were afraid to be
the first to sit down. The atmosphere is as stiltedly
grave as if they were attending a funeral service.
Their eyes keep fixed on the head of the house, who has
gone to the window at right and is staring out frowningly, savagely chewing a toothpick.*

MILLER (*finally—irritably*). Damn it, I'd ought to be

116

back at the office putting in some good licks ! I've a
whole pile of things that have got to be done to-day !

MRS. MILLER (*accusingly*). You don't mean to tell me
you're going back without seeing him ? It's your
duty—— !

MILLER (*exasperatedly*). 'Course I'm not ! I wish
you'd stop jumping to conclusions ! What else did I
come home for, I'd like to know ? Do I usually come
way back here for dinner on a busy day ? I was only
wishing this hadn't come up—just at this particular time.

(*He ends up very lamely and is irritably conscious of the fact.*)

TOMMY (*who has been fidgeting restlessly—unable to bear
the suspense a moment longer*). What is it Dick done ?
Why is everyone scared to tell me ?

MILLER (*seizes this as an escape valve—turns and fixes his
youngest son with a stern, forbidding eye*). Young man, I've
never spanked you yet, but that don't mean I never will !
Seems to me that you've been just itching for it lately !
You keep your mouth shut till you're spoken to—or I
warn you something's going to happen !

MRS. MILLER. Yes, Tommy, you keep still and don't
bother your pa. (*Then warningly to her husband.*) Careful what you say, Nat. Little pitchers have big ears.

MILLER (*peremptorily*). You kids skedaddle—all of
you. Why are you always hanging around the house ?
Go out and play in the yard, or take a walk, and get some
fresh air.

> (*Mildred takes Tommy's hand and leads him out
> through the front parlour. Arthur hangs back,
> as if the designation " kids " couldn't possibly*

> *apply to him. His father notices this—impatiently.*)

You, too, Arthur.

> (*Arthur goes out with a stiff, wounded dignity.*)

LILY (*tactfully*). I think I'll go for a walk, too.

> (*She goes out through the front parlour. Sid makes a movement as if to follow her.*)

MILLER. I'd like you to stay, Sid—for a while, anyway.

SID. Sure. (*He sits down in the rocking-chair at right, rear, of table and immediately yawns.*) Gosh, I'm dead. Don't know what's the matter with me to-day. Can't seem to keep awake.

MILLER (*with caustic sarcasm*). Maybe that demon chowder you drank at the picnic poisoned you !

> (*Sid looks sheepish and forces a grin. Then Miller turns to his wife with the air of one who determinedly faces the unpleasant.*)

Where is Richard ?

MRS. MILLER (*flusteredly*). He's still in bed. I made him stay in bed to punish him—and I thought he ought to, anyway, after being so sick. But he says he feels all right.

SID (*with another yawn*). 'Course he does. When you're young you can stand anything without it feazing you. Why, I remember when I could come down on the morning after, fresh as a daisy, and eat a breakfast of pork chops and fried onions and—— (*He stops guiltily.*)

MILLER (*bitingly*). I suppose that was before eating lobster shells had ruined your iron constitution !

MRS. MILLER (*regards her brother severely*).   If I was in your shoes, I'd keep still !   (*Then turning to her husband.*) Richard must be feeling better.   He ate all the dinner I sent up, Norah says.

MILLER.   I thought you weren't going to give him any dinner—to punish him.

MRS. MILLER (*guiltily*).   Well—in his weakened condition—I thought it best——   (*Then defensively.*)   But you needn't think I haven't punished him.   I've given him pieces of my mind he won't forget in a hurry.   And I've kept reminding him his real punishment was still to come—that you were coming home to dinner on purpose —and then he'd learn that you could be terrible stern when he did such awful things.

MILLER (*stirs uncomfortably*).   Hmm !

MRS. MILLER.   And that's just what it's your duty to do—punish him good and hard !   The idea of him daring——   (*Then hastily.*)   But you be careful how you go about it, Nat.   Remember he's like you inside —too sensitive for his own good.   And he never would have done it, I know, if it hadn't been for that darned little dunce, Muriel, and her numbskull father—and then all of us teasing him and hurting his feelings all day—and then you lost your temper and were so sharp with him right after dinner before he went out.

MILLER (*resentfully*).   I see this is going to work round to where it's all my fault !

MRS. MILLER.   Now, I didn't say that, did I ?   Don't go losing your temper again.   And here's another thing. You know as well as I, Richard would never have done such a thing alone. Why, he wouldn't know how ! He must have been influenced and led by someone.

MILLER. Yes, I believe that. Did you worm out of him who it was ? (*Then angrily.*) By God, I'll make whoever it was regret it !

MRS. MILLER. No, he wouldn't admit there was any-one. (*Then triumphantly.*) But there is one thing I did worm out of him—and I can tell you it relieved my mind more'n anything. You know, I was afraid he'd been with one of those bad women. Well, turns out there wasn't any Hedda. She was just out of those books he's been reading. He swears he's never known a Hedda in his life. And I believe him. Why, he seemed disgusted with me for having such a notion. (*Then lamely.*) So somehow—I can't kind of feel it's all as bad as I thought it was. (*Then quickly and indignantly.*) But it's bad enough, goodness knows—and you punish him good just the same. The idea of a boy of his age—— ! Shall I go up now and tell him to get dressed, you want to see him ?

MILLER (*helplessly—and irritably*). Yes ! I can't waste all day listening to you !

MRS. MILLER (*worriedly*). Now you keep your temper, Nat, remember !

(*She goes out through the front parlour.*)

MILLER. Darn women, anyway ! They always get you mixed up. Their minds simply don't know what logic is ! (*Then he notices that Sid is dozing—sharply.*) Sid !

SID (*blinking—mechanically*). I'll take the same. (*Then hurriedly.*) What'd you say, Nat ?

MILLER (*caustically*).   What I didn't say was what'll you have.   (*Irritably.*)   Do you want to be of some help, or don't you ?   Then keep awake and try and use your brains !   This is a damned sight more serious than Essie has any idea !   She thinks there weren't any girls mixed up with Richard's spree last night—but I happen to know there were !   (*He takes a letter from his pocket.*) Here's a note a woman left with one of the boys downstairs at the office this morning—didn't ask to see me, just said give me this.   He'd never seen her before— said she looked like a tart.   (*He has opened the letter and reads:*)   " Your son got the booze he drank last night at the Pleasant Beach House.   The bartender there knew he was under age but served him just the same. He thought it was a good joke to get him soused.   If you have any guts you will run that bastard out of town." Well, what do you think of that ?   It's a woman's handwriting—not signed, of course.

SID.   She's one of the babies, all right—judging from her elegant language.

MILLER.   See if you recognize the handwriting.

SID (*with a reproachful look*).   Nat, I resent the implication that I correspond with all the tramps around this town.   (*Looking at the letter.*)   No, I don't know who this one could be.   (*Handing the letter back.*)   But I deduce that the lady had a run-in with the barkeep and wants revenge.

MILLER (*grimly*).   And I deduce that before that she must have picked up Richard—or how would she know who he was ?—and took him to this dive.

SID.   Maybe.   The Pleasant Beach House is nothing

but a bed house——— (*Quickly.*) At least, so I've been told.

MILLER. That's just the sort of damned fool thing he might do to spite Muriel, in the state of mind he was in —pick up some tart. And she'd try to get him drunk so———

SID. Yes, it might have happened like that—and it might not. How're we ever going to prove it ? Everyone at the Pleasant Beach will lie their heads off.

MILLER (*simply and proudly*). Richard won't lie.

SID. Well, don't blame him if he don't remember everything that happened last night. (*Then sincerely concerned.*) I hope you're wrong, Nat. That kind of baby is dangerous for a kid like Dick—in more ways than one. You know what I mean.

MILLER (*frowningly*). Yep—and that's just what's got me worried. Damn it, I've got to have a straight talk with him—about women and all those things. I ought to have long ago.

SID. Yes. You ought.

MILLER. I've tried to a couple of times. I did it all right with Wilbur and Lawrence and Arthur, when it came time—but, hell, with Richard I always get sort of ashamed of myself and can't get started right. You feel, in spite of all his bold talk out of books, that he's so darned innocent inside.

SID. I know. I wouldn't like the job. (*Then after a pause—curiously.*) How were you figuring to punish him for his sins ?

MILLER (*frowning*). To be honest with you, Sid, I'm damned if I know. All depends on what I feel about what he feels when I first size him up—and then it'll be like shooting in the dark.

SID. If I didn't know you so well, I'd say don't be too hard on him. (*He smiles a little bitterly.*) If you remember, I was always getting punished—and see what a lot of good it did me !

MILLER (*kindly*). Oh, there's lots worse than you around, so don't take to boasting. (*Then, at a sound from the front parlour—with a sigh.*) Well, here comes the Bad Man, I guess.

SID (*getting up*). I'll beat it.

> (*But it is Mrs. Miller who appears in the doorway, looking guilty and defensive. Sid sits down again.*)

MRS. MILLER. I'm sorry, Nat—but he was sound asleep and I didn't have the heart to wake him. I waited for him to wake up but he didn't.

MILLER (*concealing a relief of which he is ashamed—exasperatedly*). Well, I'll be double damned ! If you're not the———

MRS. MILLER (*defensively aggressive*). Now don't lose your temper at me, Nat Miller ! You know as well as I do he needs all the sleep he can get to-day—after last night's ructions ! Do you want him to be taken down sick ? And what difference does it make to you, anyway ? You can see him when you come home for supper, can't you ? My goodness, I never saw you so savage-tempered ! You'd think you couldn't bear waiting to punish him ?

MILLER (*outraged*). Well, I'll be eternally——
(*Then suddenly he laughs.*) No use talking, you certainly take the cake ! But you know darned well I told you I'm not coming home to supper to-night. I've got a date with Jack Lawson that may mean a lot of new advertising and it's important.

MRS. MILLER. Then you can see him when you do come home.

MILLER (*covering his evident relief at this respite with a fuming manner*). All right ! All right ! I give up ! I'm going back to the office. (*He starts for the front parlour.*) Bring a man all the way back here on a busy day and then you—— No consideration——

(*He disappears, and a moment later the front door is heard shutting behind him.*)

MRS. MILLER. Well ! I never saw Nat so bad-tempered.

SID (*with a chuckle*). Bad temper, nothing. He's so tickled to get out of it for a while he can't see straight !

MRS. MILLER (*with a sniff*). I hope I know him better than you. (*Then fussing about the room, setting this and that in place, while Sid yawns drowsily and blinks his eyes.*) Sleeping like a baby—so innocent-looking. You'd think butter wouldn't melt in his mouth. It all goes to show you never can tell by appearances—not even when it's your own child. The idea !

SID (*drowsily*). Oh, Dick's all right, Essie. Stop worrying.

MRS. MILLER (*with a sniff*). Of course, you'd say that.

I suppose you'll have him out with you painting the town red the next thing !

(*As she is talking, Richard appears in the doorway from the sitting-room. He shows no ill effects from his experience the night before. In fact, he looks surprisingly healthy. He is dressed in old clothes that look as if they had been hurriedly flung on. His expression is one of hang-dog guilt mingled with a defensive defiance.*)

RICHARD (*with self-conscious unconcern, ignoring his mother*). Hello, Sid.

MRS. MILLER (*whirls on him*). What are you doing here, Young Man ? I thought you were asleep ! Seems to me you woke up pretty quick—just after your pa left the house !

RICHARD (*sulkily*). I wasn't asleep. I heard you in the room.

MRS. MILLER (*outraged*). Do you mean to say you were deliberately deceiving——

RICHARD. I wasn't deceiving. You didn't ask if I was asleep.

MRS. MILLER. It amounts to the same thing and you know it ! It isn't enough your wickedness last night, but now you have to take to lying !

RICHARD. I wasn't lying, Ma. If you'd asked if I was asleep I'd have said no.

MRS. MILLER. I've a good mind to send you straight back to bed and make you stay there !

RICHARD. Ah, what for, Ma ? It was only giving me a headache, lying there.

MRS. MILLER. If you've got a headache, I guess you know it doesn't come from that ! And imagine me standing there, and feeling sorry for you, like a fool— even having a run-in with your pa because—— But you wait till he comes back to-night ! If you don't catch it !

RICHARD (*sulkily*). I don't care.

MRS. MILLER. You don't care ? You talk as if you weren't sorry for what you did last night !

RICHARD (*defiantly*). I'm not sorry.

MRS. MILLER. Richard ! You ought to be ashamed ! I'm beginning to think you're hardened in wickedness, that's what !

RICHARD (*with bitter despondency*). I'm not sorry because I don't care a darn what I did, or what's done to me, or anything about anything ! I won't do it again——

MRS. MILLER (*seizing on this to relent a bit*). Well, I'm glad to hear you say that, anyway !

RICHARD. But that's not because I think it was wicked or any such old-fogy moral notion, but because it wasn't any fun. It didn't make me happy and funny like it does Uncle Sid——

SID (*drowsily*). What's that ? Who's funny ?

RICHARD (*ignoring him*). It only made me sadder— and sick—so I don't see any sense in it.

MRS. MILLER. Now you're talking sense ! That's a good boy.

RICHARD. But I'm not sorry I tried it once—curing the soul by means of the senses, as Oscar Wilde says.

(*Then with despairing pessimism.*)   But what does it matter what I do or don't do ?   Life is all a stupid farce !   I'm through with it !   (*With a sinister smile.*)   It's lucky there aren't any of General Gabler's pistols around—or you'd see if I'd stand it much longer !

MRS. MILLER (*worriedly impressed by this threat—but pretending scorn*).   I don't know anything about General Gabler—I suppose that's more of those darned books—but you're a silly gabbler yourself when you talk that way !

RICHARD (*darkly*).   That's how little you know about me.

MRS. MILLER (*giving in to her worry*).   I wish you wouldn't say those terrible things—about life and pistols ! You don't want to worry me to death, do you ?

RICHARD (*reassuringly stoical now*).   You needn't worry, Ma.   It was only my despair talking.   But I'm not a coward.   I'll face—my fate.

MRS. MILLER (*stands looking at him puzzledly—then gives it up with a sigh*).   Well, all I can say is you're the queerest boy I ever did hear of !   (*Then solicitously, putting her hand on his forehead.*)   How's your headache ?   Do you want me to get you some Bromo Seltzer ?

RICHARD (*taken down—disgustedly*).   No, I don't ! Aw, Ma, you don't understand anything !

MRS. MILLER.   Well, I understand this much : It's your liver, that's what !   You'll take a good dose of salts to-morrow morning, and no nonsense about it !   (*Then suddenly.*)   My goodness, I wonder what time it's getting to be.   I've got to go upstreet.   (*She goes to the front-*

parlour doorway—then turns.) You stay here, Richard, you hear ? Remember you're not allowed out to-day—for a punishment.

> *(She hurries away. Richard sits in tragic gloom. Sid, without opening his eyes, speaks to him drowsily.)*

SID. Well, how's my fellow Rum Pot, as good old Dowie calls us ? Got a head ?

RICHARD *(startled—sheepishly).* Aw, don't go dragging that up, Uncle Sid. I'm never going to be such a fool again, I tell you.

SID *(with drowsy cynicism—not unmixed with bitterness at the end).* Seems to me I've heard someone say that before. Who could it have been, I wonder ? Why, if it wasn't Sid Davis ! Yes, sir, I've heard him say that very thing a thousand times, must be. But then he's always fooling ; you can't take a word he says seriously ; he's a card, that Sid is !

RICHARD *(darkly).* I was desperate, Uncle—even if she wasn't worth it. I was wounded to the heart.

SID. I like to the quick better myself—more stylish. *(Then sadly.)* But you're right. Love is hell on a poor sucker. Don't I know it ?

> *(Richard is disgusted and disdains to reply. Sid's chin sinks on his chest and he begins to breathe noisily, fast asleep. Richard glances at him with aversion. There is a sound of someone on the porch and the screen door is opened and Mildred enters. She smiles on seeing her uncle, then gives a start on seeing Richard.)*

MILDRED. Hello ! Are you allowed up ?

RICHARD. Of course, I'm allowed up.

MILDRED (*comes and sits in her father's chair at right, front, of table*). How did Pa punish you ?

RICHARD. He didn't. He went back to the office without seeing me.

MILDRED. Well, you'll catch it later. (*Then rebukingly.*) And you ought to. If you'd ever seen how awful you looked last night !

RICHARD. Ah, forget it, can't you ?

MILDRED. Well, are you ever going to do it again, that's what I want to know.

RICHARD. What's that to you ?

MILDRED (*with suppressed excitement*). Well, if you don't solemnly swear you won't—then I won't give you something I've got for you.

RICHARD. Don't try to kid me. You haven't got anything.

MILDRED. I have, too.

RICHARD. What ?

MILDRED. Wouldn't you like to know ! I'll give you three guesses.

RICHARD (*with disdainful dignity*). Don't bother me. I'm in no mood to play riddles with kids !

MILDRED. Oh, well, if you're going to get snippy ! Anyway, you haven't promised yet.

RICHARD (*a prey to keen curiosity now*). I promise.
What is it ?

MILDRED. What would you like best in the world ?

RICHARD. I don't know. What ?

MILDRED. And you pretend to be in love ! If I told
Muriel that !

RICHARD (*breathlessly*). Is it—from her ?

MILDRED (*laughing*). Well, I guess it's a shame to keep
you guessing. Yes. It is from her. I was walking
past her place just now when I saw her waving from their
parlour window, and I went up and she said give this to
Dick, and she didn't have a chance to say anything else
because her mother called her and said she wasn't allowed
to have company. So I took it—and here it is. (*She
gives him a letter folded many times into a tiny square.
Richard opens it with a trembling eagerness and reads.
Mildred watches him curiously—then sighs affectedly.*) Gee,
it must be nice to be in love like you are—all with one
person.

RICHARD (*his eyes shining*). Gee, Mid, do you know
what she says—that she didn't mean a word in that other
letter. Her old man made her write it. And she loves
me and only me and always will, no matter how they
punish her !

MILDRED. My ! I'd never think she had that much
spunk.

RICHARD. Huh ! You don't know her ! Think I
could fall in love with a girl that was afraid to say her soul's
her own ? I should say not ! (*Then more gleefully still.*)
And she's going to try and sneak out and meet me to-

night. She says she thinks she can do it. (*Then suddenly feeling this enthusiasm before Mildred is entirely the wrong note for a cynical pessimist—with an affected bitter laugh.*) Ha ! I knew darned well she couldn't hold out—that she'd ask to see me again. (*He misquotes cynically.*) " Women never know when the curtain has fallen. They always want another act."

MILDRED. Is that so, Smarty ?

RICHARD (*as if he were weighing the matter*). I don't know whether I'll consent to keep this date or not.

MILDRED. Well, I know ! You're not allowed out, you silly ! So you can't !

RICHARD (*dropping all pretense—defiantly*). Can't I, though ! You wait and see if I can't ! I'll see her to-night if it's the last thing I ever do ! I don't care how I'm punished after !

MILDRED (*admiringly*). Goodness ! I never thought you had such nerve !

RICHARD. You promise to keep your face shut, Mid —until after I've left—then you can tell Pa and Ma where I've gone—I mean, if they're worrying I'm off like last night.

MILDRED. All right. Only you've got to do something for me when I ask.

RICHARD. 'Course I will. (*Then excitedly.*) And say, Mid ! Right now's the best chance for me to get away—while everyone's out ! Ma'll be coming back soon and she'll keep watching me like a cat—— (*He starts for the back parlour.*) I'm going. I'll sneak out the back.

MILDRED (*excitedly*). But what'll you do till night-time ? It's ages to wait.

RICHARD. What do I care how long I wait ! (*Intensely sincere now.*) I'll think of her—and dream ! I'd wait a million years and never mind it—for her ! (*He gives his sister a superior scornful glance.*) The trouble with you is, you don't understand what love means !

> (*He disappears through the back parlour. Mildred looks after him admiringly. Sid puffs and begins to snore peacefully.*)

CURTAIN

SCENE TWO

SCENE. *A strip of beach along the harbour. At left, a bank of dark earth, running half-diagonally back along the beach, marking the line where the sand of the beach ends and fertile land begins. The top of the bank is grassy and the trailing boughs of willow trees extend out over it and over a part of the beach. At left, front, is a path leading up the bank, between the willows. On the beach, at centre, front, a white, flat-bottomed rowboat is drawn up, its bow about touching the bank, the painter trailing up the bank, evidently made fast to the trunk of a willow. Half-way down the sky, at rear, left, the crescent of the new moon casts a soft, mysterious, caressing light over everything. The sand of the beach shimmers palely. The forward half (left of centre) of the rowboat is in the deep shadow cast by the willow, the stern section is in moonlight. In the dis-*

tance, the orchestra of a summer hotel can be heard very faintly at intervals.

Richard is discovered sitting sideways on the gunwale of the rowboat near the stern. He is facing left, watching the path. He is in a great state of anxious expectancy, squirming about uncomfortably on the narrow gunwale, kicking at the sand restlessly, twirling his straw hat, with a bright-coloured band in stripes, around on his finger.

RICHARD (*thinking aloud*). Must be nearly nine. . . . I can hear the Town Hall clock strike, it's so still to-night . . . Gee, I'll bet Ma had a fit when she found out I'd sneaked out . . . I'll catch hell when I get back, but it'll be worth it . . . if only Muriel turns up . . . she didn't say for certain she could . . . gosh, I wish she'd come ! . . . am I sure she wrote nine ? . . . (*He puts the straw hat on the seat amidships and pulls the folded letter out of his pocket and peers at it in the moonlight.*) Yes, it's nine, all right. (*He starts to put the note back in his pocket, then stops and kisses it—then shoves it away hastily, sheepish, looking around him shamefacedly, as if afraid he were being observed.*) Aw, that's silly . . . no, it isn't either . . . not when you're really in love. . . . (*He jumps to his feet restlessly.*) Darn it, I wish she'd show up ! . . . think of something else . . . that'll make the time pass quicker . . . where was I this time last night ? . . . waiting outside the Pleasant Beach House . . . Belle . . . ah, forget her ! . . . now, when Muriel's coming . . . that's a fine time to think of—— ! . . . but you hugged and kissed her . . . not until I was drunk, I didn't . . . and then it was all showing off . . . darned fool ! . . . and I didn't go upstairs with her . . . even if she was pretty . . .

aw, she wasn't pretty . . . she was all painted up . . . she was just a whore . . . she was everything dirty . . . Muriel's a million times prettier anyway . . . Muriel and I will go upstairs . . . when we're married . . . but that will be beautiful . . . but I oughtn't even to think of that yet . . . it's not right . . . I'd never—now . . . and she'd never . . . she's a decent girl . . . I couldn't love her if she wasn't . . . but after we're married. . . . (*He gives a little shiver of passionate longing—then resolutely turns his mind away from these improper, almost desecrating thoughts.*) That damned barkeep kicking me . . . I'll bet you if I hadn't been drunk I'd have given him one good punch in the nose, even if he could have licked me after ! . . . (*Then with a shiver of shamefaced revulsion and self-disgust.*) Aw, you deserved a kick in the pants . . . making such a darned slob of yourself . . . reciting the Ballad of Reading Gaol to those lowbrows ! . . . you must have been a fine sight when you got home ! . . . having to be put to bed and getting sick ! . . . Phaw ! . . . (*He squirms disgustedly.*) Think of something else, can't you ? . . . recite something . . . see if you remember . . .

" Nay, let us walk from fire unto fire,
    From passionate pain to deadlier delight—
    I am too young to live without desire,
    Too young art thou to waste this summer night———"

. . . gee, that's a peach ! . . . I'll have to memorize the rest and recite it to Muriel the next time. . . . I wish I could write poetry . . . about her and me. . . . (*He sighs and stares around him at the night.*) Gee, it's beautiful to-night . . . as if it was a special night . . . for me and Muriel. . . . Gee, I love to-night. . . . I

love the sand, and the trees, and the grass, and the water
and the sky, and the moon . . . it's all in me and I'm
in it . . . God, it's so beautiful ! (*He stands staring at
the moon with a rapt face. From the distance the Town
Hall clock begins to strike. This brings him back to earth
with a start.*) There's nine now. . . . (*He peers at
the path apprehensively.*) I don't see her . . . she must
have got caught. . . . (*Almost tearfully.*) Gee, I hate
to go home and catch hell . . . without having seen her !
. . . (*Then calling a manly cynicism to his aid.*) Aw, who
ever heard of a woman ever being on time. . . . I
ought to know enough about life by this time not to
expect . . . (*Then with sudden excitement.*) There she
comes now. . . . Gosh ! (*He heaves a huge sigh of
relief—then recites dramatically to himself, his eyes on the
approaching figure.*)

" And lo my love, mine own soul's heart, more dear
    Than mine own soul, more beautiful than God,
    Who hath my being between the hands of her———"

(*Then hastily.*) Mustn't let her know I'm so tickled.
. . . I ought to be about that first letter, anyway . . .
if women are too sure of you, they treat you like slaves
. . . let her suffer, for a change. . . . (*He starts to
stroll around with exaggerated carelessness, turning his back
on the path, hands in pockets, whistling with insouciance
" Waiting at the Church."*

> (*Muriel McComber enters from down the path, left
> front. She is fifteen, going on sixteen. She
> is a pretty girl with a plump, graceful little
> figure, fluffy, light-brown hair, big naïve won-
> dering dark eyes, a round, dimpled face, a
> melting drawly voice. Just now she is in a*

135

*great thrilled state of timid adventurousness.
She hesitates in the shadow at the foot of the
path, waiting for Richard to see her ; but he
resolutely goes on whistling with back turned,
and she has to call him.*)

MURIEL. Oh, Dick !

RICHARD (*turns around with an elaborate simulation of
being disturbed in the midst of profound meditation*). Oh,
hello. Is it nine already ? Gosh, time passes—when
you're thinking.

MURIEL (*coming toward him as far as the edge of the
shadow—disappointedly*). I thought you'd be waiting
right here at the end of the path. I'll bet you'd forgotten I was even coming.

RICHARD (*strolling a little toward her but not too far—
carelessly*). No, I hadn't forgotten, honest. But I got
to thinking about life.

MURIEL. You might think of me for a change, after
all the risk I've run to see you ! (*Hesitating timidly on
the edge of the shadow.*) Dick ! You come here to me.
I'm afraid to go out in that bright moonlight where
anyone might see me.

RICHARD (*coming toward her—scornfully*). Aw, there
you go again—always scared of life !

MURIEL (*indignantly*). Dick Miller, I do think you've
got an awful nerve to say that after all the risks I've run
making this date and then sneaking out ! You didn't
take the trouble to sneak any letter to me, I notice !

RICHARD. No, because after your first letter, I thought
everything was dead and past between us.

MURIEL. And I'll bet you didn't care one little bit ! (*On the verge of humiliated tears.*) Oh, I was a fool ever to come here ! I've got a good notion to go right home and never speak to you again ! (*She half turns back toward the path.*)

RICHARD (*frightened—immediately becomes terribly sincere—grabbing her hand*). Aw, don't go, Muriel ! Please ! I didn't mean anything like that, honest I didn't ! Gee, if you knew how broken-hearted I was by that first letter, and how darned happy your second letter made me—— !

MURIEL (*happily relieved—but appreciates she has the upper hand now and doesn't relent at once*). I don't believe you.

RICHARD. You ask Mid how happy I was. She can prove it.

MURIEL. She'd say anything you told her to. I don't care anything about what she'd say. It's you. You've got to swear to me——

RICHARD. I swear !

MURIEL (*demurely*). Well then, all right, I'll believe you.

RICHARD (*his eyes on her face lovingly—genuine adoration in his voice*). Gosh, you're pretty to-night, Muriel ! It seems ages since we've been together ! If you knew how I've suffered—— !

MURIEL. I did, too.

RICHARD (*unable to resist falling into his tragic literary pose for a moment*). The despair in my soul—— (*He recites dramatically :*) " Something was dead in each of us,

137

And what was dead was Hope ! " That was me ! My hope of happiness was dead ! (*Then with sincere boyish fervour.*) Gosh, Muriel, it sure is wonderful to be with you again ! (*He puts a timid arm around her awkwardly.*)

MURIEL (*shyly*). I'm glad—it makes you happy. I'm happy, too.

RICHARD. Can't I—won't you let me kiss you—now ? Please ! (*He bends his face toward hers.*)

MURIEL (*ducking her head away—timidly*). No. You mustn't. Don't——

RICHARD. Aw, why can't I ?

MURIEL. Because—I'm afraid.

RICHARD (*discomfited—taking his arm from around her—a bit sulky and impatient with her*). Aw, that's what you always say ! You're always so afraid ! Aren't you ever going to let me ?

MURIEL. I will—sometime.

RICHARD. When ?

MURIEL. Soon, maybe.

RICHARD. To-night, will you ?

MURIEL (*coyly*). I'll see.

RICHARD. Promise ?

MURIEL. I promise—maybe.

RICHARD. All right. You remember you've promised. (*Then coaxingly :*) Aw, don't let's stand here. Come on out and we can sit down in the boat.

MURIEL (*hesitantly*). It's so bright out there.

RICHARD. No one'll see. You know there's never anyone around here at night.

MURIEL (*illogically*). I know there isn't. That's why I thought it would be the best place. But there might be someone.

RICHARD (*taking her hand and tugging at it gently*). There isn't a soul. (*Muriel steps out a little and looks up and down fearfully. Richard goes on insistently.*) Aw, what's the use of a moon if you can't see it !

MURIEL. But it's only a new moon. That's not much to look at.

RICHARD. But I want to see you. I can't here in the shadow. I want to—drink in—all your beauty.

MURIEL (*can't resist this*). Well, all right—only I can't stay only a few minutes. (*She lets him lead her toward the stern of the boat.*)

RICHARD (*pleadingly*). Aw, you can stay a little while, can't you ? Please ! (*He helps her in and she settles herself in the stern seat of the boat, facing diagonally left front.*)

MURIEL. A little while. (*He sits beside her.*) But I've got to be home in bed again pretending to be asleep by ten o'clock. That's the time Pa and Ma come up to bed, as regular as clockwork, and Ma always looks into my room.

RICHARD. But you'll have oodles of time to do that.

MURIEL (*excitedly*). Dick, you have no idea what I went through to get here to-night ! My, but it was exciting ! You know Pa's punishing me by sending me to bed at eight sharp, and I had to get all undressed and into bed 'cause at half-past he sends Ma up to make sure I've obeyed, and she came up, and I pretended to be asleep, and she went down again, and I got up and dressed in such a hurry—I must look a sight, don't I ?

RICHARD. You do not ! You look wonderful !

MURIEL. And then I sneaked down the back stairs. And the pesky old stairs squeaked, and my heart was in my mouth, I was so scared, and then I sneaked out through the back yard, keeping in the dark under the trees, and—— My, but it was exciting ! Dick, you don't realize how I've been punished for your sake. Pa's been so mean and nasty, I've almost hated him !

RICHARD. And you don't realize what I've been through for you—and what I'm in for—for sneaking out—— (*Then darkly.*) And for what I did last night —what your letter made me do !

MURIEL (*made terribly curious by his ominous tone*). What did my letter make you do ?

RICHARD (*beginning to glory in this*). It's too long a story—and let the dead past bury its dead. (*Then with real feeling.*) Only it isn't past, I can tell you ! What I'll catch when Pa gets hold of me !

MURIEL. Tell me, Dick ! Begin at the beginning and tell me !

RICHARD (*tragically*). Well, after your old—your father left our place I caught holy hell from Pa.

MURIEL. Dick ! You mustn't swear !

RICHARD (*sombrely*). Hell is the only word that can describe it. And on top of that, to torture me more, he gave me your letter. After I'd read that I didn't want to live any more. Life seemed like a tragic farce.

MURIEL. I'm so awful sorry, Dick—honest I am ! But you might have known I'd never write that unless——

RICHARD. I thought your love for me was dead. I thought you'd never loved me, that you'd only been cruelly mocking me—to torture me !

MURIEL. Dick ! I'd never ! You know I'd never !

RICHARD. I wanted to die. I sat and brooded about death. Finally I made up my mind I'd kill myself.

MURIEL (*excitedly*). Dick ! You didn't !

RICHARD. I did, too ! If there'd been one of Hedda Gabler's pistols around, you'd have seen if I wouldn't have done it beautifully ! I thought, when I'm dead, she'll be sorry she ruined my life !

MURIEL (*cuddling up a little to him*). If you ever had ! I'd have died, too ! Honest, I would !

RICHARD. But suicide is the act of a coward. That's what stopped me. (*Then with a bitter change of tone.*) And anyway, I thought to myself, she isn't worth it.

MURIEL (*huffily*). That's a nice thing to say !

RICHARD. Well, if you meant what was in that letter, you wouldn't have been worth it, would you ?

MURIEL. But I've told you Pa——

RICHARD. So I said to myself, I'm through with women ; they're all alike !

MURIEL. I'm not.

RICHARD. And I thought, what difference does it make what I do now ? I might as well forget her and lead the pace that kills, and drown my sorrows ! You

know I had eleven dollars saved up to buy you something for your birthday, but I thought, she's dead to
me now and why shouldn't I throw it away ? (*Then
hastily.*) I've still got almost five left, Muriel, and I can
get you something nice with that.

MURIEL (*excitedly*). What do I care about your old
presents ? You tell me what you did !

RICHARD (*darkly again*). After it was dark, I sneaked
out and went to a low dive I know about.

MURIEL. Dick Miller, I don't believe you ever !

RICHARD. You ask them at the Pleasant Beach House
if I didn't ! They won't forget me in a hurry !

MURIEL (*impressed and horrified*). You went there ?
Why, that's a terrible place ! Pa says it ought to be
closed by the police !

RICHARD (*darkly*). I said it was a dive, didn't I ?
It's a " secret house of shame." And they let me into a
secret room behind the bar-room. There wasn't anyone
there but a Princeton Senior I know—he belongs to
Tiger Inn and he's full-back on the football team—and
he had two chorus girls from New York with him, and
they were all drinking champagne.

MURIEL (*disturbed by the entrance of the chorus girls*).
Dick Miller ! I hope you didn't notice——

RICHARD (*carelessly*). I had a highball by myself and
then I noticed one of the girls—-the one that wasn't with
the full-back—looking at me. She had strange-looking
eyes. And then she asked me if I wouldn't drink champagne with them and come and sit with her.

MURIEL. She must have been a nice thing ! (*Then a bit falteringly*.) And did—you ?

RICHARD (*with tragic bitterness*). Why shouldn't I, when you'd told me in that letter you'd never see me again ?

MURIEL (*almost tearfully*). But you ought to have known Pa made me——

RICHARD. I didn't know that then. (*Then rubbing it in*.) Her name was Belle. She had yellow hair—the kind that burns and stings you !

MURIEL. I'll bet it was dyed !

RICHARD. She kept smoking one cigarette after another—but that's nothing for a chorus girl.

MURIEL (*indignantly*). She was low and bad, that's what she was or she couldn't be a chorus girl, and her smoking cigarettes proves it ! (*Then falteringly again*.) And then what happened ?

RICHARD (*carelessly*). Oh, we just kept drinking champagne—I bought a round—and then I had a fight with the barkeep and knocked him down because he'd insulted her. He was a great big thug but——

MURIEL (*huffily*). I don't see how he could—insult that kind ! And why did you fight for her ? Why didn't the Princeton full-back who'd brought them there ? He must have been bigger than you.

RICHARD (*stopped for a moment—then quickly*). He was too drunk by that time.

MURIEL. And were you drunk ?

RICHARD. Only a little then. I was worse later. (*Proudly.*) You ought to have seen me when I got home ! I was on the verge of delirium tremens!

MURIEL. I'm glad I didn't see you. You must have been awful. I hate people who get drunk. I'd have hated you !

RICHARD. Well, it was all your fault, wasn't it ? If you hadn't written that letter——

MURIEL. But I've told you I didn't mean—— (*Then faltering but fascinated.*) But what happened with that Belle—after—before you went home ?

RICHARD. Oh, we kept drinking champagne and she said she'd fallen in love with me at first sight and she came and sat on my lap and kissed me.

MURIEL (*stiffening*). Oh !

RICHARD (*quickly, afraid he has gone too far*). But it was only all in fun, and then we just kept on drinking champagne, and finally I said good night and came home.

MURIEL. And did you kiss her ?

RICHARD. No, I didn't.

MURIEL (*distractedly*). You did, too ! You're lying and you know it. You did, too ! (*Then tearfully.*) And there I was right at that time lying in bed not able to sleep, wondering how I was ever going to see you again and crying my eyes out, while you——! (*She suddenly jumps to her feet in a tearful fury.*) I hate you ! I wish you were dead ! I'm going home this minute ! I never want to lay eyes on you again ! And this time I mean it !

144

(She tries to jump out of the boat, but he holds her back. All the pose has dropped from him now and he is in a frightened state of contrition.)

RICHARD *(imploringly).* Muriel ! Wait ! Listen !

MURIEL. I don't want to listen ! Let me go ! If you don't I'll bite your hand !

RICHARD. I won't let you go ! You've got to let me explain ! I never——— ! Ouch !

(For Muriel has bitten his hand and it hurts, and, stung by the pain, he lets go instinctively, and she jumps quickly out of the boat and starts running toward the path. Richard calls after her with bitter despair and hurt.)

All right ! Go if you want to—if you haven't the decency to let me explain ! I hate you, too ! I'll go and see Belle !

MURIEL *(seeing he isn't following her, stops at the foot of the path—defiantly).* Well, go and see her—if that's the kind of girl you like ! What do I care ? *(Then as he only stares before him broodingly, sitting dejectedly in the stern of the boat, a pathetic figure of injured grief.)* You can't explain ! What can you explain ? You owned up you kissed her !

RICHARD. I did not. I said she kissed me.

MURIEL *(scornfully, but drifting back a step in his direction).* And I suppose you just sat and let yourself be kissed ! Tell that to the Marines !

RICHARD *(injuredly).* All right ! If you're going to call me a liar every word I say———

145

MURIEL (*drifting back another step*). I didn't call you a liar. I only meant—it sounds fishy. Don't you know it does ?

RICHARD. I don't know anything. I only know I wish I was dead !

MURIEL (*gently reproving*). You oughtn't to say that. It's wicked. (*Then after a pause.*) And I suppose you'll tell me you didn't fall in love with her ?

RICHARD (*scornfully*). I should say not ! Fall in love with that kind of girl ! What do you take me for ?

MURIEL (*practically*). How do you know what you did if you drank so much champagne ?

RICHARD. I kept my head—with her. I'm not a sucker, no matter what you think !

MURIEL (*drifting nearer*). Then you didn't—love her ?

RICHARD. I hated her ! She wasn't even pretty ! And I had a fight with her before I left, she got so fresh. I told her I loved you and never could love anyone else, and for her to leave me alone.

MURIEL. But you said just now you were going to see her——

RICHARD. That was only bluff. I wouldn't—unless you left me. Then I wouldn't care what I did—any more than I did last night. (*Then suddenly defiant.*) And what if I did kiss her once or twice ? I only did it to get back at you !

MURIEL. Dick !

RICHARD. You're a fine one to blame me—when it was all your fault ! Why can't you be fair ? Didn't

I think you were out of my life for ever ?   Hadn't you written me you were ?   Answer me that !

MURIEL.   But I've told you a million times that Pa——

RICHARD.   Why didn't you have more sense than to let him make you write it ?   Was it my fault you didn't ?

MURIEL.   It was your fault for being so stupid !   You ought to have known he stood right over me and told me each word to write.   If I'd refused, it would only have made everything worse.   I had to pretend, so I'd get a chance to see you.   Don't you see, Silly ?   And I had sand enough to sneak out to meet you to-night, didn't I ? (*He doesn't answer.   She moves nearer.*)   Still I can see how you felt the way you did—and maybe I am to blame for that.   So I'll forgive and forget, Dick—if you'll swear to me you didn't even think of loving that——

RICHARD (*eagerly*).   I didn't !   I swear, Muriel.   I couldn't.   I love you !

MURIEL.   Well, then—I still love you.

RICHARD.   Then come back here, why don't you ?

MURIEL (*coyly*).   It's getting late.

RICHARD.   It's not near half-past yet.

MURIEL (*comes back and sits down by him shyly*).   All right—only I'll have to go soon, Dick.   (*He puts his arm around her.   She cuddles up close to him.*)   I'm sorry—I hurt your hand.

RICHARD.   That was nothing.   It felt wonderful—even to have you bite !

MURIEL (*impulsively takes his hand and kisses it*).

There ! That'll cure it. (*She is overcome by confusion at her boldness.*)

RICHARD. You shouldn't—waste that—on my hand. (*Then tremblingly.*) You said—you'd let me——

MURIEL. I said, maybe.

RICHARD. Please, Muriel. You know—I want it so !

MURIEL. Will it wash off—her kisses—make you forget you ever—for always ?

RICHARD. I should say so ! I'd never remember —anything but it—never want anything but it—ever again.

MURIEL (*shyly lifting her lips*). Then—all right—Dick. (*He kisses her tremblingly and for a moment their lips remain together. Then she lets her head sink on his shoulder and sighs softly.*) The moon *is* beautiful, isn't it ?

RICHARD (*kissing her hair*). Not as beautiful as you ! Nothing is ! (*Then after a pause.*) Won't it be wonderful when we're married ?

MURIEL. Yes—but it's so long to wait.

RICHARD. Perhaps I needn't go to Yale. Perhaps Pa will give me a job. Then I'd soon be making enough to——

MURIEL. You better do what your pa thinks best— and I'd like you to be at Yale. (*Then patting his face.*) Poor you ! Do you think he'll punish you awful ?

RICHARD (*intensely*). I don't know and I don't care ! Nothing would have kept me from seeing you to-night —not if I'd had to crawl over red-hot coals ! (*Then falling back on Swinburne—but with passionate sincerity.*)

148

You have my being between the hands of you ! You are " my love, mine own soul's heart, more dear than mine own soul, more beautiful than God ! "

MURIEL (*shocked and delighted*). Ssshh ! It's wrong to say that.

RICHARD (*adoringly*). Gosh, but I love you ! Gosh, I love you—Darling !

MURIEL. I love you, too—Sweetheart !

> (*They kiss. Then she lets her head sink on his shoulder again and they both sit in a rapt trance, staring at the moon.*)

(*After a pause—dreamily.*) Where'll we go on our honeymoon, Dick ? To Niagara Falls ?

RICHARD (*scornfully*). That dump where all the silly fools go ? I should say not ! (*With passionate romanticism.*) No, we'll go to some far-off wonderful place ! (*He calls on Kipling to help him.*) Somewhere out on the Long Trail—the trail that is always new—on the road to Mandalay ! We'll watch the dawn come up like thunder out of China !

MURIEL (*hazily but happily*). That'll be wonderful, won't it ?

CURTAIN

SCENE THREE

SCENE. *The sitting-room of the Miller house again—about
10 o'clock the same night. Miller is sitting in his rocker
at left, front, of table, his wife in the rocker at right,
front, of table. Moonlight shines through the screen*

door at right, rear. Only the green-shaded reading lamp is lit and by its light Miller, his specs on, is reading a book while his wife, sewing basket in lap, is working industriously on a doily. Mrs. Miller's face wears an expression of unworried content. Miller's face has also lost its look of harassed preoccupation, although he still is a prey to certain misgivings, when he allows himself to think of them. Several books are piled on the table by his elbow, the books that have been confiscated from Richard.

MILLER (*chuckles at something he reads—then closes the book and puts it on the table. Mrs. Miller looks up from her sewing*). This Shaw's a comical cuss—even if his ideas are so crazy they oughtn't to allow them to be printed. And that Swinburne's got a fine swing to his poetry—if he'd only choose some other subjects besides loose women.

MRS. MILLER (*smiling teasingly*). I can see where you're becoming corrupted by those books, too—pretending to read them out of duty to Richard, when your nose has been glued to the page !

MILLER. No, no—but I've got to be honest. There's something to them. That Rubaiyat of Omar Khayyám, now. I read that over again and liked it even better than I had before—parts of it, that is, where it isn't all about boozing.

MRS. MILLER (*has been busy with her own thoughts during this last—with a deep sigh of relief*). My, but I'm glad Mildred told me where Richard went off to. I'd have worried my heart out if she hadn't. But now, it's all right.

MILLER (*frowning a little*). I'd hardly go so far as to

say that. Just because we know he's all right to-night doesn't mean last night is wiped out. He's still got to be punished for that.

MRS. MILLER (*defensively*). Well, if you ask me, I think after the way I punished him all day, and the way I know he's punished himself, he's had about all he deserves. I've told you how sorry he was, and how he said he'd never touch liquor again. It didn't make him feel happy like Sid, but only sad and sick, so he didn't see anything in it for him.

MILLER. Well, if he's really got that view of it driven into his skull, I don't know but I'm glad it all happened. That'll protect him more than a thousand lectures—just horse sense about himself. (*Then frowning again.*) Still, I can't let him do such things and go scot-free. And then ; besides, there's another side to it—— (*He stops abruptly.*)

MRS. MILLER (*uneasily*). What do you mean, another side ?

MILLER (*hastily*). I mean, discipline. There's got to be some discipline in a family. I don't want him to get the idea he's got a stuffed shirt at the head of the table. No, he's got to be punished, if only to make the lesson stick in his mind, and I'm going to tell him he can't go to Yale, seeing he's so undependable.

MRS. MILLER (*up in arms at once*). Not go to Yale ! I guess he can go to Yale ! Every man of your means in town is sending his boys to college ! What would folks think of you ? You let Wilbur go, and you'd have let Lawrence, only he didn't want to, and you're letting Arthur ! If our other children can get the benefit of a college education, you're not going to pick on Richard——

MILLER. Hush up, for God's sake ! If you'd let me finish what I started to say ! I said I'd *tell* him that now——bluff——then later on I'll change my mind, if he behaves himself.

MRS. MILLER. Oh well, if that's all—— (*Then defensively again.*) But it's your duty to give him every benefit. He's got an exceptional brain, that boy has ! He's proved it by the way he likes to read all those deep plays and books and poetry.

MILLER. But I thought you—— (*He stops, grinning helplessly.*)

MRS. MILLER. You thought I what ?

MILLER. Never mind.

MRS. MILLER (*sniffs, but thinks it better to let this pass*). You mark my words, that boy's going to turn out to be a great lawyer, or a great doctor, or a great writer, or——

MILLER (*grinning*). You agree he's going to be great, anyway.

MRS. MILLER. Yes, I most certainly have a lot of faith in Richard.

MILLER. Well, so have I, as far as that goes.

MRS. MILLER (*after a pause—judicially*). And as for his being in love with Muriel, I don't see but what it might work out real well. Richard could do worse.

MILLER. But I thought you had no use for her, thought she was stupid.

MRS. MILLER. Well, so I did, but if she's good for Richard and he wants her—— (*Then inconsequentially.*) Ma used to say you weren't overbright, but she changed her mind when she saw I didn't care if you were or not.

MILLER (*not exactly pleased by this*). Well, I've been bright enough to——

MRS. MILLER (*going on as if he had not spoken*). And Muriel's real cute-looking, I have to admit that. Takes after her mother. Alice Briggs was the prettiest girl before she married.

MILLER. Yes, and Muriel will get big as a house after she's married, the same as her mother did. That's the trouble. A man never can tell what he's letting himself in for—— (*He stops, feeling his wife's eyes fixed on him with indignant suspicion.*)

MRS. MILLER (*sharply*). I'm not too fat and don't you say it !

MILLER. Who was talking about you ?

MRS. MILLER. And I'd rather have some flesh on my bones than be built like a string bean and bore a hole in a chair every time I sat down—like some people !

MILLER (*ignoring the insult—flatteringly*). Why, no one'd ever call you fat, Essie. You're only plump, like a good figure ought to be.

MRS. MILLER (*childishly pleased—gratefully giving tit for tat*). Well, you're not skinny, either—only slender—and I think you've been putting on weight lately, too.

> (*Having thus squared matters she takes up her sewing again. A pause. Then Miller asks incredulously.*)

MILLER. You don't mean to tell me you're actually taking this Muriel crush of Richard's seriously, do you? I know it's a good thing to encourage right now but—pshaw, why, Richard'll probably forget all about her before he's away six months, and she'll have forgotten him.

MRS. MILLER. Don't be so cynical. (*Then, after a pause, thoughtfully.*) Well, anyway, he'll always have it to remember—no matter what happens after—and that's something.

MILLER. You bet that's something. (*Then with a grin.*) You surprise me at times with your deep wisdom.

MRS. MILLER. You don't give me credit for ever having common sense, that's why. (*She goes back to her sewing.*)

MILLER (*after a pause*). Where'd you say Sid and Lily had gone off to?

MRS. MILLER. To the beach to listen to the band. (*She sighs sympathetically.*) Poor Lily! Sid'll never change, and she'll never marry him. But she seems to get some queer satisfaction out of fussing over him like a hen that's hatched a duck—though Lord knows I wouldn't in her shoes!

MILLER. Arthur's up with Elsie Rand, I suppose?

MRS. MILLER. Of course.

MILLER. Where's Mildred?

MRS. MILLER. Out walking with her latest. I've forgot who it is. I can't keep track of them. (*She smiles.*)

MILLER (*smiling*). Then, from all reports, we seem to be completely surrounded by love !

MRS. MILLER. Well, we've had our share, haven't we ? We don't have to begrudge it to our children. (*Then has a sudden thought.*) But I've done all this talking about Muriel and Richard and clean forgot how wild old McComber was against it. But he'll get over that, I suppose.

MILLER (*with a chuckle*). He has already. I ran into him upstreet this afternoon and he was meek as pie. He backed water and said he guessed I was right. Richard had just copied stuff out of books, and kids would be kids, and so on. So I came off my high horse a bit—but not too far—and I guess all that won't bother anyone any more. (*Then rubbing his hands together—with a boyish grin of pleasure.*) And I told you about getting that business from Lawson, didn't I ? It's been a good day, Essie—a darned good day !

> (*From the hall beyond the front parlour the sound of the front door being opened and shut is heard. Mrs. Miller leans forward to look, pushing her specs up.*)

MRS. MILLER (*in a whisper*). It's Richard.

MILLER (*immediately assuming an expression of becoming gravity*). Hmm.

> (*He takes off his spectacles and puts them back in their case and straightens himself in his chair. Richard comes slowly in from the front parlour. He walks like one in a trance, his eyes shining with a dreamy happiness, his spirit still too exalted to be conscious of his surroundings, or*

*to remember the threatened punishment. He
carries his straw hat dangling in his hand,
quite unaware of its existence.*)

RICHARD (*dreamily, like a ghost addressing fellow shades*).
Hello.

MRS. MILLER (*staring at him worriedly*). Hello, Richard.

MILLER (*sizing him up shrewdly*). Hello, Son.

(*Richard moves past his mother and comes to the far
corner, left front, where the light is dimmest,
and sits down on the sofa, and stares before
him, his hat dangling in his hand.*)

MRS. MILLER (*with frightened suspicion now*). Goodness, he acts queer ! Nat, you don't suppose he's
been———— ?

MILLER (*with a reassuring smile*). No. It's love, not
liquor, this time.

MRS. MILLER (*only partly reassured—sharply*). Richard !
What's the matter with you ? (*He comes to himself with
a start. She goes on scoldingly.*) How many times have
I told you to hang up your hat in the hall when you come
in ! (*He looks at his hat as if he were surprised at its existence. She gets up fussily and goes to him.*) Here. Give
it to me. I'll hang it up for you this once. And what
are you sitting over here in the dark for ? Don't forget
your father's been waiting to talk to you !

(*She comes back to the table and he follows her, still
half in a dream, and stands by his father's
chair. Mrs. Miller starts for the hall with
his hat.*)

156

MILLER (*quietly but firmly now*). You better leave Richard and me alone for a while, Essie.

MRS. MILLER (*turns to stare at him apprehensively*). Well—all right. I'll go sit on the piazza. Call me if you want me. (*Then a bit pleadingly.*) But you'll remember all I've said, Nat, won't you ?

> (*Miller nods reassuringly. She disappears through the front parlour. Richard, keenly conscious of himself as the about-to-be-sentenced criminal by this time, looks guilty and a bit defiant, searches his father's expressionless face with uneasy side glances, and steels himself for what is coming.*)

MILLER (*casually, indicating Mrs. Miller's rocker*). Sit down, Richard.

> (*Richard slumps awkwardly into the chair and sits in a self-conscious, unnatural position. Miller sizes him up keenly—then suddenly smiles and asks with quiet mockery.*)

Well, how are the vine leaves in your hair this evening ?

RICHARD (*totally unprepared for this approach—shamefacedly mutters*). I don't know, Pa.

MILLER. Turned out to be poison ivy, didn't they ? (*Then kindly.*) But you needn't look so alarmed. I'm not going to read you any temperance lecture. That'd bore me more than it would you. And, in spite of your damn foolishness last night, I'm still giving you credit for having brains. So I'm pretty sure anything I could say to you you've already said to yourself.

RICHARD (*his head down—humbly*). I know I was a darned fool.

MILLER (*thinking it well to rub in this aspect—disgustedly*). You sure were—not only a fool but a downright, stupid, disgusting fool !

(*Richard squirms, his head still lower.*)

It was bad enough for you to let me and Arthur see you, but to appear like that before your mother and Mildred ——— ! And I wonder if Muriel would think you were so fine if she ever saw you as you looked and acted then. I think she'd give you your walking papers for keeps. And you couldn't blame her. No nice girl wants to give her love to a stupid drunk !

RICHARD (*writhing*). I know, Pa.

MILLER (*after a pause—quietly*). All right. Then that settles—the booze end of it. (*He sizes Richard up searchingly—then suddenly speaks sharply.*) But there is another thing that's more serious. How about that tart you went to bed with at the Pleasant Beach House ?

RICHARD (*flabbergasted—stammers*). You know——— ? But I didn't ! If they've told you about her down there, they must have told you I didn't ! She wanted me to —but I wouldn't. I gave her the five dollars just so she'd let me out of it. Honest, Pa, I didn't ! She made everything seem rotten and dirty—and—I didn't want to do a thing like that to Muriel—no matter how bad I thought she'd treated me—even after I felt drunk, I didn't. Honest !

MILLER. How'd you happen to meet this lady, anyway ?

RICHARD. I can't tell that, Pa. I'd have to snitch on someone—and you wouldn't want me to do that.

MILLER (*a bit taken aback*). No. I suppose I wouldn't. Hmm. Well, I believe you—and I guess that settles that. (*Then, after a quick, furtive glance at Richard, he nerves himself for the ordeal and begins with a shamefaced, self-conscious solemnity.*) But listen here, Richard, it's about time you and I had a serious talk about—hmm—certain matters pertaining to—and now that the subject's come up of its own accord, it's good time—I mean, there's no use in procrastinating further—so, here goes.

> (*But it doesn't go smoothly and as he goes on he becomes more and more guiltily embarrassed and self-conscious and his expressions more stilted. Richard sedulously avoids even glancing at him, his own embarrassment made tenfold more painful by his father's.*)

Richard, you have now come to the age when—— Well, you're a fully developed man, in a way, and it's only natural for you to have certain desires of the flesh, to put it that way—— I mean, pertaining to the opposite sex—certain natural feelings and temptations—that'll want to be gratified—and you'll want to gratify them. Hmm—well, human society being organized as it is, there's only one outlet for—unless you're a scoundrel and go around ruining decent girls—which you're not, of course. Well, there are a certain class of women—always have been and always will be as long as human nature is what it is—— It's wrong, maybe, but what can you do about it? I mean, girls like that one you—girls there's something doing with—and lots of 'em are pretty, and it's human nature if you—— But that doesn't mean to ever get mixed up with them seriously! You just have what you want and pay 'em and forget it. I know that sounds hard and unfeeling, but we're talking facts and—— But don't think I'm encouraging you to—— If you can stay away from 'em, all the better— but if—why—hmm—— Here's what I'm driving at, Richard. They're apt to be whited sepulchres—I mean, your whole life might be ruined if—so, darn it, you've got to know how to—— I mean, there are ways and means—— (*Suddenly he can go no farther and winds up helplessly.*) But, hell, I suppose you boys talk all this over among yourselves and you know more about it than I do. I'll admit I'm no authority. I never had any-thing to do with such women, and it'll be a hell of a lot better for you if you never do !

RICHARD (*without looking at him*). I'm never going to, Pa. (*Then shocked indignation coming into his voice.*) I don't see how you could think I could—now—when you know I love Muriel and am going to marry her. I'd die before I'd—— !

MILLER (*immensely relieved—enthusiastically*). That's the talk ! By God, I'm proud of you when you talk like that ! (*Then hastily.*) And now that's all of that. There's nothing more to say and we'll forget it, eh ?

RICHARD (*after a pause*). How are you going to punish me, Pa ?

MILLER. I *was* sort of forgetting that, wasn't I ? Well, I'd thought of telling you you couldn't go to Yale——

RICHARD (*eagerly*). Don't I have to go ? Gee, that's great ! Muriel thought you'd want me to. I was tell-ing her I'd rather you gave me a job on the paper because then she and I could get married sooner. (*Then with a boyish grin.*) Gee, Pa, you picked a lemon. That isn't any punishment. You'll have to do something besides that.

MILLER (*grimly—but only half concealing an answering grin*). Then you'll go to Yale and you'll stay there till you graduate, that's the answer to that ! Muriel's got good sense and you haven't ! (*Richard accepts this philosophically.*) And now we're finished, you better call your mother.

> (*Richard opens the screen door and calls "Ma," and a moment later she comes in. She glances quickly from son to husband and immediately knows that all is well and tactfully refrains from all questions.*)

MRS. MILLER. My, it's a beautiful night. The moon's way down low—almost setting.

> (*She sits in her chair and sighs contentedly. Richard remains standing by the door, staring out at the moon, his face pale in the moonlight.*)

MILLER (*with a nod at Richard, winking at his wife*). Yes, I don't believe I've hardly ever seen such a beautiful night—with such a wonderful moon. Have you, Richard ?

RICHARD (*turning to them—enthusiastically*). No ! It was wonderful—down at the beach—— (*He stops abruptly, smiling shyly.*)

MILLER (*watching his son—after a pause—quietly*). I can only remember a few nights that were as beautiful as this—and they were long ago, when your mother and I were young and planning to get married.

RICHARD (*stares at him wonderingly for a moment, then*

quickly from his father to his mother and back again, strangely, as if he'd never seen them before——then he looks almost disgusted and swallows as if an acrid taste had come into his mouth——but then suddenly his face is transfigured by a smile of shy understanding and sympathy. He speaks shyly). Yes, I'll bet those must have been wonderful nights, too. You sort of forget the moon was the same way back then —and everything.

MILLER (*huskily*). You're all right, Richard. (*He gets up and blows his nose.*)

MRS. MILLER (*fondly*). You're a good boy, Richard.

(*Richard looks dreadfully shy and embarrassed at this. His father comes to his rescue.*)

MILLER. Better get to bed early to-night, Son, hadn't you ?

RICHARD. I couldn't sleep. Can't I go out on the piazza and sit for a while——until the moon sets ?

MILLER. All right. Then you better say good night now. I don't know about your mother, but I'm going to bed right away. I'm dead tired.

MRS. MILLER. So am I.

RICHARD (*goes to her and kisses her*). Good night, Ma.

MRS. MILLER. Good night. Don't you stay up till all hours now.

RICHARD (*comes to his father and stands awkwardly before him*). Good night, Pa.

MILLER (*puts his arm around him and gives him a hug*). Good night, Richard.

(Richard turns impulsively and kisses him—then hurries out the screen door. Miller stares after him—then says huskily.)

First time he's done that in years. I don't believe in kissing between fathers and sons after a certain age— seems mushy and silly—but that meant something ! And I don't think we'll ever have to worry about his being safe—from himself—again. And I guess no matter what life will do to him, he can take care of it now. *(He sighs with satisfaction and, sitting down in his chair, begins to unlace his shoes.)* My darned feet are giving me fits !

MRS. MILLER *(laughing)*. Why do you bother unlacing your shoes now, you big goose—when we're going right up to bed ?

MILLER *(as if he hadn't thought of that before, stops)*. Guess you're right. *(Then getting to his feet—with a grin.)* Mind if I don't say my prayers to-night, Essie ? I'm certain God knows I'm too darned tired.

MRS. MILLER. Don't talk that way. It's real sinful. *(She gets up—then laughing fondly.)* If that isn't you all over ! Always looking for an excuse to—— You're worse than Tommy ! But all right. I suppose to-night you needn't. You've had a hard day. *(She puts her hand on the reading-lamp switch.)* I'm going to turn out the light. All ready ?

MILLER. Yep. Let her go, Gallagher. *(She turns out the lamp. In the ensuing darkness the faint moonlight shines full in through the screen door. Walking together toward the front parlour they stand full in it for a moment, looking out. Miller puts his arm around her. He says in a low voice.*)   There he is—like a statue of Love's Young Dream.   (*Then he sighs and speaks with a gentle nostalgic melancholy.*)   What's it that Rubaiyat says :

" Yet Ah, that Spring should vanish with the Rose !
   That Youth's sweet-scented manuscript should close ! "

(*Then throwing off his melancholy, with a loving smile at her.*) Well, Spring isn't everything, is it, Essie ?   There's a lot to be said for Autumn.   That's got beauty, too.   And Winter—if you're together.

MRS. MILLER (*simply*).   Yes, Nat.

> (*She kisses him and they move quietly out of the moonlight, back into the darkness of the front parlour.*)

CURTAIN

Days Without End

A Modern Miracle Play

to
CARLOTTA

Scenes

ACT ONE

PLOT FOR A NOVEL

Scene : John Loving's office in the offices of Eliot and Company, New York City—an afternoon in early Spring, 1932.

ACT TWO

PLOT FOR A NOVEL (*continued*)

Scene : Living-room of the Lovings' duplex apartment —later the same afternoon.

ACT THREE

PLOT FOR A NOVEL (*continued*)

Scene One : The living-room again—evening of the same day.
Scene Two : John Loving's study—later that night.

ACT FOUR

THE END OF THE END

Scene One : The study and Elsa's bedroom—a little before dawn of a day about a week later.
Scene Two : The interior of a church—a few minutes later.

5

Characters

(In the order in which they appear)

JOHN
LOVING
WILLIAM ELIOT
FATHER MATTHEW BAIRD
ELSA, *John Loving's wife*
MARGARET
LUCY HILLMAN
DR. HERBERT STILLWELL
NURSE

6

ACT ONE
PLOT FOR A NOVEL

SCENE. *John Loving's private office in the offices of Eliot and Company, New York City. On the left, a window. Before it, a chair, its back to the window, and a table. At rear of table, an armchair, facing front. A third chair is at right of table. In the rear wall, a door leading to the outer offices. At centre of the room, toward right, another chair.*

It is afternoon of a cloudy day in Spring, 1932. The light from the window is chill and grey. At the rise of the curtain, this light is concentrated around the two figures seated at the table. As the action goes on, the light imperceptibly spreads until, at the close of the opening scene between John and Loving, it has penetrated to all parts of the room.

John is seated in the chair at left of desk. He is forty, of medium height. His face is handsome, with the rather heavy, conventional American type of good looks——a straight nose and a square jaw, a wide mouth that has an incongruous feminine sensitiveness, a broad forehead, blue eyes. He is dressed in a dark suit, white shirt and collar, a dark tie, black shoes and socks.

Loving sits in the armchair at rear of table. He is the same age, of the same height and figure, is dressed in every detail exactly the same. His hair is the same ——dark, streaked with grey. In contrast to this

7

similarity between the two, there is an equally strange dissimilarity. For Loving's face is a mask whose features reproduce exactly the features of John's face— the death mask of a John who has died with a sneer of scornful mockery on his lips. And this mocking scorn is repeated in the expression of the eyes which stare bleakly from behind the mask.

John nervously writes a few words on a pad—then stops abruptly and stares before him. Loving watches him.

LOVING (*his voice singularly toneless and cold but at the same time insistent*). Surely, you don't need to make any more notes for the second part—your hero's manhood up to the time he (*a sneer comes into his voice*) at last finds love. I should think you could remember that— only too well.

JOHN (*mechanically*). Yes.

LOVING (*sneeringly*). As for the third part, I know you have the most vivid recollection of his terrible sin.

JOHN. Don't mock, damn you !

LOVING. So it's only in the last part that you will have to use your imagination. How are you going to end this interesting plot of yours ? Given your hero's ridiculous conscience, what happens then ?

JOHN. He has the courage to confess—and she forgives.

LOVING. The wish is father to that thought, eh ? A pretty, sentimental ending—but a bit too pointed, don't you think ? I'm afraid she might begin to wonder——

JOHN (*apprehensively*).   Yes.   That's true.

LOVING.   I advise you to make the last part so obviously fictitious that it will kill any suspicion which might be aroused by what has gone before.

JOHN.   How can I end it, then ?

LOVING (*after a second's pause—in a voice he tries to make casual but which is indefinitely sinister*).   Why not have the wife die ?

JOHN (*starts—with a shudder*).   Damn you !   What makes you think of that ?

LOVING.   Why, nothing—except I thought you'd agreed that the further removed from present actuality you make your ending, the better it will be.

JOHN.   Yes—but——

LOVING (*mockingly*).   I hope you don't suspect some hidden, sinister purpose behind my suggestion.

JOHN.   I don't know.   I feel—— (*Then as if desperately trying to shake off his thoughts.*)   No !   I won't think of it !

LOVING.   And I was thinking, too, that it would be interesting to work out your hero's answer to his problem, if his wife died, and imagine what he would do with his life then.

JOHN.   No !   Damn you, stop making me think—— !

LOVING.   Afraid to face your ghosts—even by proxy ? Surely, even you can have that much courage !

JOHN.   It is dangerous—to call things.

LOVING.   Still   superstitious ?   Well,   I   hope   you

9

realize I'm only trying to encourage you to make something of this plot of yours more significant—for your soul, shall I say ?—than a cowardly trick !

JOHN. You know it's more than that. You know I'm doing it to try and explain to myself, as well as to her.

LOVING (*sneeringly*). To excuse yourself to yourself, you mean ! To lie and escape admitting the obvious natural reason for——

JOHN. You lie ! I want to get at the real truth and understand what was behind—-what evil spirit of hate possessed me to make me—

LOVING (*contemptuously—but as he goes on a strange defiant note of exultance comes into his voice*). So it's come back to that again, eh ? Your old familiar nightmare ! You poor, damned superstitious fool ! I tell you again what I have always told you : There is nothing—nothing to hope for, nothing to fear—neither devils nor gods —nothing at all !

> (*There is a knock on the door at rear. John immediately pretends to be writing. At the same time his features automatically assume the meaninglessly affable expression which is the American business man's welcoming poker face. Loving sits motionlessly regarding him with scornful eyes.*)

JOHN (*without looking up, calls*). Come in.

> (*The door in rear is half opened and William Eliot, John Loving's partner, looks in. He is about forty, stout, with a prematurely bald head, a round face, a humorous, good-natured mouth, small eyes behind horn-rimmed spectacles.*)

ELIOT. Hello, John. Busy?

JOHN. Foolish question, Bill.

ELIOT (*his eyes pass over Loving without seeing him. He does not see him now or later. He sees and hears only John, even when Loving speaks. And it will be so with all the characters. They are quite unaware of Loving's existence, although at times one or another may subtly sense his presence. Eliot comes forward. He says jokingly*). You sound downhearted, John. Don't let our little depression get you. There's always the poorhouse. Quite cosy, too, they say. Peace for the weary—

LOVING (*cuts in—mockingly*). There is much to be said for peace.

ELIOT (*as if it were John who had spoken*). Yes, John, there sure is—these damned days. (*Then giving John a glance of concern.*) Look here. I think our troubles are getting your nerve. You've seemed worn ragged lately. Why not take a few days in the country?

JOHN. Nonsense! I'm fine. (*Forcing a humorous tone.*) What, besides the poorhouse, is on your mind, Bill?

ELIOT. Nothing but lunch. Ate too much again, damn it. What were you doping out when I came in? Got some new scheme for us?

JOHN. No.

LOVING. Merely trying to work out the answer to a puzzle—a human puzzle.

JOHN (*hurriedly*). That is, I'm playing around with a plot for a novel that's come into my mind lately.

ELIOT (*with amused surprise*). What? Good God, don't tell me the literary bug is biting you again? I thought you'd got that out of your system long ago when you got engaged to Elsa and decided to come in with me and make some money.

JOHN. Well, I thought I might as well do something with all this leisure. Oh, I'll probably never write it, but it's amusing to dope out.

ELIOT. Why shouldn't you write it? You certainly showed you could write in the old days—articles, anyway. (*Then with a grin.*) Why, I can remember when I couldn't pick up an advanced-thinker organ without running into a red-hot article of yours denouncing Capitalism or religion or something.

JOHN (*smiling good-naturedly*). You always did have a mean memory, Bill.

ELIOT (*laughs*). God, John, how you've changed! What hymns of hate you used to emit against poor old Christianity! Why, I remember one article where you actually tried to prove that no such figure as Christ had ever existed.

LOVING (*his tone suddenly cold and hostile*). I still feel the same on that subject.

ELIOT (*gives John a surprised glance*). Feel? Can't understand anyone having feelings any more on such a dead issue as religion.

JOHN (*confused*). Well, to tell the truth, I haven't given it a thought in years, but—— (*Then hurriedly.*) But, for Pete's sake, let's not get started on religion.

ELIOT (*changes the subject tactfully*). Tell me about this novel of yours, John. What's it all about?

JOHN. Nothing to tell yet. I haven't got it finally worked out.

LOVING. The most important part, that is—the end.

JOHN (*in a joking tone*). But when I have, Bill, I'll be only too glad to get your esteemed criticism.

ELIOT. That's a promise, remember—— (*Then getting up.*) Well, I suppose I better get back to my office. (*He starts for the door—then turns back.*) Oh, I knew there was something I'd forgotten to tell you. Lucy Hillman called up while you were out.

JOHN (*carelessly*). Yes? What did she want?

ELIOT. Wanted you. Got my office by mistake. She'll call up later. It was important, she said to tell you.

JOHN. Her idea of important! Probably wants my advice on what to give Walter for a birthday present.

ELIOT. What the devil's got into Walter lately, anyway? Getting drunk as a pastime may have its points, but as an exclusive occupation—— Not to mention all his affairs with women. How does Lucy stand it? But I hear she's going to pieces, too.

JOHN. I don't believe it. She isn't the kind to have affairs.

ELIOT. I don't mean that. I mean booze.

JOHN. Oh! Well, if it's true, you can hardly blame her.

13

ELIOT. There are children, aren't there? Why hasn't she the guts to divorce him?

JOHN. Don't ask me. We haven't seen much of Lucy, either, for a long time. (*He dismisses the subject by looking down at his pad, as if he wanted to start writing.*)

ELIOT (*taking the hint*). Well, I'll move along.

JOHN. See you later, Bill.

(*Eliot goes out, rear. After the door closes behind him John speaks tensely.*)

Why did she phone? Important, she said. What can have happened?

LOVING (*coldly*). Who knows? But you know very well she can't be trusted. You'd better be prepared for any stupid folly. And better get the end of your novel decided upon, so you can tell your plot—before it's too late.

JOHN (*tensely*). Yes.

LOVING (*the hidden sinister note again creeping into his coldly casual tone*). There can be only one sensible, logical end for your hero, after he has lost his wife for ever— that is, provided he loves her as much as he boasts to himself he does—and if he has any honour or courage left!

JOHN (*gives a start—then bitterly*). Ah! I see now what you're driving at! And you talk of courage and honour! (*Defiantly.*) No! He must go on! He must find a faith—somewhere!

LOVING (*an undercurrent of anger in his sneering*). Somewhere, eh? Now I wonder what hides behind that somewhere ? Is it your old secret weakness—the cowardly yearning to go back—— ?

JOHN (*defensively*). I don't know what you're thinking about.

LOVING. You lie ! I know you ! And I'll make you face it in the end of your story—face it and kill it, finally and for ever !

> (*There is again a knock on the door and John's eyes go to his pad. This time Eliot comes in immediately, without waiting for an answer.*)

JOHN. Hello, Bill. What's up now ?

ELIOT (*comes forward, a twinkle in his eye*). John, there's a mysterious visitor outside demanding to see you.

JOHN. You mean—Lucy ?

ELIOT. Lucy ? No. This is a man. He ran into me before he got to Miss Sims and asked for you. (*Grinning.*) And as it's liable to be a bitter blow, I thought I better break the news in person.

JOHN. What's the joke ? Who is it ?

ELIOT. It's a priest.

JOHN. A priest ?

LOVING (*harshly*). I don't know any priests ! Tell him to get out !

ELIOT. Now don't be disrespectful. He claims he's your uncle.

JOHN. My uncle ? Did he give his name ?

ELIOT. Yes. Father Baird. Said he'd just got in from the West.

JOHN (*dumbfounded—forcing a smile*). Well, I'll be damned.

ELIOT (*laughs*). My God, think of you having a priest for an uncle ! That's too rich !

JOHN. I haven't seen him since I was a boy.

ELIOT. Why so scared ? Afraid he's come to lecture you on your sins ?

LOVING (*angrily*). He may be a joke to you. He's not to me, damn him !

ELIOT (*gives John a surprised, disapproving glance*). Oh, come, John. Not as bad as that, is it ? He struck me as a nice old guy.

JOHN (*hurriedly*). He is. I didn't mean that. I always liked him. He was very kind to me when I was a kid. He acted as my guardian for a while. But I wish he'd given me warning. (*Then picking up the telephone.*) Well, it's rotten to keep him cooling his heels. Hello. Send Father Baird in.

ELIOT (*turning to the door*). I'll get out.

JOHN. No, as a favour, stay around until the ice is broken.

> (*He has gotten up and is going toward the door. Loving remains in his chair, his eyes fixed before him in a hostile stare, his body tensed defensively.*)

ELIOT. Sure.

(*A knock comes on the door. John opens it and Father Matthew Baird enters. He is seventy, about John and Loving's height, erect, robust, with thick white hair, ruddy complexion. There is a clear resemblance to John and Loving in the general cast of his features and the colour of his eyes. His appearance and personality radiate health and observant kindliness—also the confident authority of one who is accustomed to obedience and deference—and one gets immediately from him the sense of an unshakable inner calm and certainty, the peace of one whose goal in life is fixed by an end beyond life.*)

JOHN (*constrained and at the same time affectionate*). Hello, Uncle ! What in the world brings you——

FATHER BAIRD (*clasping John's hand in a strong grip*). Jack ! (*His manner is very much what it must have been when John was a boy and he was the guardian. Deeply moved, he puts his arm around John and gives him an affectionate hug.*) My dear Jack ! This is—— (*He sees Eliot and stops, a bit embarrassed.*)

JOHN (*moved and embarrassed, getting away from his arm*). I want you to meet my partner—Bill Eliot—my uncle, Father Baird.

ELIOT. It's a great pleasure, Father.

FATHER BAIRD (*shakes his hand—a formal, old-fashioned courtesy in his manner*). The pleasure is mine, Mr. Eliot. But I feel I've had the privilege of your acquaintance already through Jack's letters.

JOHN. Sit down, Uncle. (*He indicates the chair at*

17

*right of desk. Father Baird sits down. John sits in his
chair at left. Eliot stands by the chair at right, centre.)*

ELIOT. Well, I'll leave you two alone and pretend to
be busy. That's the hardest job we have now, Father
—keeping up the pretence of work.

FATHER BAIRD. You have plenty of company, if
that's any consolation. I get the same tale of woe from
everyone in our part of the country.

ELIOT. I'm afraid the company doesn't console a bit.
They're all too darned whiny.

FATHER BAIRD (*a twinkle coming into his eye*). Ah, who
can blame you for whining when your omnipotent
Golden Calf explodes into sawdust before your adoring
eyes right at the height of his deification? It's tragic,
no other word—unless the word be comic.

LOVING (*his voice a mocking sneer*). And what salvation for us are you preaching? The Second Coming?

FATHER BAIRD (*startled, turns to stare at John. Eliot
also looks at him, surprised and disapproving of this taunt.
Father Baird says quietly, without any sign of taking offence*).
The First Coming is enough, Jack—for those who
remember it. (*Then he turns to Eliot—in a joking tone.*)
If you knew how familiar that note sounds from him,
Mr. Eliot. Here I've been feeling strange, looking at
him and seeing what a big man of affairs he'd grown, and
saying to myself, can this be my old Jack? And then
he has to go and give himself away with a strain of his
old bold whistling in the dark, and I see he's still only
out of short pants a while, as I knew him last! (*He
gives a comic sigh of relief.*) Thank you, Jack. I feel
quite at home with you now.

ELIOT (*immensely amused, especially at the expression of boyish discomfiture on John's face—laughingly*). John, I begin to feel sorry for you. You've picked on some one out of your class.

FATHER BAIRD (*with a wink at Eliot*). Did you hear him throw the word preaching in my face, Mr. Eliot —with a dirty sneer in his voice? There's injustice for you. If you knew what a burden he made my life for years with his preaching. Letter upon letter—each with a soap box enclosed, so to speak. The plague began right after I'd had to go West and leave him to his own devices. He was about to pass out of my guardianship and go to college with the bit of money his parents had left for him when he reached eighteen. So I had to let him go his own way. I'd learned it was no use fighting him, anyway. I'd done that and found it was a great satisfaction to him and only made him worse. And I had faith, if let alone, he'd come back to his senses in the end.

LOVING (*sneeringly*). And how mistaken you were in that faith!

FATHER BAIRD (*without turning—quietly*). No. The end isn't yet, Jack. (*He goes on to Eliot with a renewal of his humorously complaining tone.*) You wouldn't believe what a devil's advocate he was in those days, Mr. Eliot.

ELIOT. You needn't tell me, Father. I was his classmate. He organized an Atheists' Club—or tried to— and almost got fired for it.

FATHER BAIRD. Yes, I remember his writing to boast about that. Well, you can appreciate then what I went through, even if he didn't write you letters.

ELIOT. But he delivered harangues, Father, when he could get anybody to listen !

FATHER BAIRD (*pityingly*). Ah, that must have been cruel, too. Mr. Eliot, I feel drawn to you. We've been through the same frightful trials.

JOHN (*with a boyishly discomfited air*). I hope you're having a good time, you two.

FATHER BAIRD (*ignoring him*). Not a moment's peace did he give me. I was the heathen to him and he was bound he'd convert me to something. First it was Atheism unadorned. Then it was Atheism wedded to Socialism. But Socialism proved too weak-kneed a mate, and the next I heard Atheism was living in free love with Anarchism, with a curse by Nietzsche to bless the union. And then came the Bolshevik dawn, and he greeted that with unholy howls of glee and wrote me he'd found a congenial home at last in the bosom of Karl Marx. He was particularly delighted when he thought they'd abolished love and marriage, and he couldn't contain himself when the news came they'd turned naughty schoolboys and were throwing spitballs at Almighty God and had supplanted Him with the slave-owning State—the most grotesque god that ever came out of Asia!

ELIOT (*chuckling*). I recognize all this, Father. I used to read his articles, as I was reminding him just before you came.

FATHER BAIRD. Don't I know them ! Didn't he send me every one with blue pencil underlinings ! But to get back to my story : Thinks I at this juncture, well, he's run away as far as he can get in that direction. Where will he hide himself next ?

LOVING (*stiffening in his chair—with angry resentment*). Run away. You talk as if I were afraid of something. Hide? Hide from what?

FATHER BAIRD (*without turning—quietly*). Don't you know, Jack? Well, if you don't yet, you will some day. (*Again to Eliot.*) I knew Communism wouldn't hold him long—and it didn't. Soon his letters became full of pessimism, and disgust with all sociological nostrums. Then followed a long silence. And what do you think was his next hiding place? Religion, no less —but as far away as he could run from home—in the defeatist mysticism of the East. First it was China and Lao Tze that fascinated him, but afterwards he ran on to Buddha, and his letters for a time extolled passionless contemplation so passionately that I had a mental view of him regarding his navel frenziedly by the hour and making nothing of it!

(*Eliot laughs and John chuckles sheepishly in spite of himself. Loving stares before him with a cold, angry disdain.*)

ELIOT. Gosh, I'm sorry I missed that! When was all this, Father?

FATHER BAIRD. In what I'd call his middle hide-and-go-seek period. But the next I knew, he was through with the East. It was not for the Western soul, he decided, and he was running through Greek philosophy and found a brief shelter in Pythagoras and numerology. Then came a letter which revealed him bogged down in evolutionary scientific truth again—a dyed-in-the-wool mechanist. That was the last I heard of his perigrinations—and, thank heaven, it was long ago. I enjoyed a long interval of peace from his missionary zeal, until finally he wrote me he was married. That letter was full of more ardent hymns of praise for a mere living woman than he'd ever written before about any of his great spiritual discoveries. And ever since then I've heard nothing but the praises of Elsa—in which I know I'll be ready to join after I've met her.

JOHN (*his face lighting up*). You bet you will! We can agree on that, at least.

FATHER BAIRD (*with a wink at Eliot*). He seems to be fixed in his last religion. I hope so. The only constant faith I've found in him before was his proud belief in himself as a bold Antichrist. (*He gives John a side glance, half smiling and half reproachful.*) Ah, well, it's a rocky road full of twists and blind alleys, isn't it, Jack —this running away from truth in order to find it? I mean, until the road finally turns back toward home.

LOVING (*with harsh defiance*). You believe I——? (*Then sneeringly.*) But, of course, you would read that into it.

JOHN (*bursts out irritably, as if he couldn't control his nerves*). But don't you think I'm about exhausted as a subject, Uncle? I do. (*He gets up nervously and moves around and stands behind Loving's chair, his hands on the back of the chair, his face directly above Loving's masked one.*)

ELIOT (*gives the priest an amused smile*). Well, I'll get back to my office. (*Father Baird gets up and he shakes his hand heartily.*) I hope we'll meet again, Father. Are you here for long?

FATHER BAIRD. Only a few days, I'm afraid.

JOHN (*coming around to them*). I'll fix up something

with Elsa for the four of us, Bill—as soon as she's feeling stronger. We won't let him run away in a few days, now we've got him here.

ELIOT. Fine! See you again, then, Father. (*He goes toward the door.*)

FATHER BAIRD. I hope so, Mr. Eliot. Good day to you.

ELIOT (*with the door open, turns back with a grin*). I feel it my duty, Father, to warn you that John's got writer's itch again. He's going to give us a novel. (*He laughs and closes the door behind him. John frowns and gives his uncle a quick uneasy glance.*)

JOHN (*indicating the chair at right, centre*). Take that chair, Uncle. It's more comfortable.

> (*He sits down in the chair at right of table where Father Baird had sat, while the priest sits in the one at right, centre. Father Baird gives him a puzzled, concerned look, as if he were trying to figure something out. Then he speaks casually.*)

FATHER BAIRD. A novel? Is that right, Jack?

JOHN (*without looking at him*). Thinking of it—to pass the time.

FATHER BAIRD. Then, judging from your letters, it ought to be a love story.

JOHN. It is—a love story.

LOVING (*mockingly*). About God's love for us!

FATHER BAIRD (*quietly rebuking*). Jack! (*A pause of*

23

silence. Father Baird gives John a quick glance again— then casually.) If you've any appointments, don't stand on ceremony ; just shoo me out.

JOHN (*turns to him shamefacedly*). Don't talk that way, Uncle. You know I wouldn't——(*with a natural, boyishly affectionate smile*). You know darned well how tickled I am to have you here.

FATHER BAIRD. I hope you're half as glad as I am to see you, Jack. (*He sighs.*) It has been a long time—too long.

JOHN. Yes. (*Smiling.*) But I'm still flabbergasted. I never dreamed you—— Why didn't you wire me you were coming ?

FATHER BAIRD. Oh, I thought I'd surprise you. (*He smiles.*) To tell you the truth, I confess I had a sneaking Sherlock Holmes desire to have a good look at you before you were expecting it.

JOHN (*frowning—uneasily*). Why ? Why should you ?

FATHER BAIRD. Well, I suppose because, not having seen you, I'm afraid that to me you were still the boy I'd known, and I was still your suspicious guardian.

JOHN (*relieved—with a boyish grin*). Oh ! I see.

FATHER BAIRD. And now I have seen you, I still must admit that the grey in your hair is lost on me, and I can't get it out of my head you're the same old Jack.

JOHN (*grinning with a boyish discomfiture*). Yes, and the devil of it is you make me feel that way, too. It's an unfair advantage, Uncle.

24

(*Father Baird laughs and John joins in.*)

FATHER BAIRD. Well, I never took unfair advantage of you in the old days, did I ?

JOHN. You certainly didn't. When I look back, I'm amazed you could have been so fair. (*Quickly—changing the subject.*) But you haven't told me yet how you happened to come East.

FATHER BAIRD (*a bit evasively*). Oh, I decided a vacation was due me. And I've had a great longing for some time to see you again.

JOHN. I only wish I could have you stay with us, but there's no room. But you must have dinner with us to-night, and every night you're here, of course.

FATHER BAIRD. Yes, I'd like to see all of you I can. But there's this, Jack. You spoke to Mr. Eliot as if Elsa were ill.

JOHN. Oh, it's nothing serious. She's just getting over the flu, and still feels a bit low.

FATHER BAIRD. Then I'd better not come to-night.

JOHN. You better had or she'll never forgive you— or me !

FATHER BAIRD. Very well. I'm only too happy.

(*A pause. He glances at John again with a
curious puzzled fixity. John catches his eyes, is
held by them for a moment, then looks away
almost furtively.*)

JOHN (*forcing a smile*). Is that the suspicious guardian look ? I've forgotten.

25

FATHER BAIRD (*as if to himself—slowly*). I feel——
(*Then suddenly.*) There's something I want to tell you,
Jack. (*A stern note comes into his voice.*) But first give
me your word of honour there will be no cheap sneering.

JOHN (*stares at him, taken aback—then quietly*). There
won't be.

FATHER BAIRD. Well, it's often come to me in the
past that I shouldn't have let you get so far from me,
that I might be in part responsible for your continued
estrangement from your Faith.

LOVING (*with mocking scorn*). My faith?

JOHN. You know that's nonsense, Uncle.

LOVING. You have always nobly done your duty.
You've never let a letter pass without some pious reminder
of my fall—with the calm assurance that I would again
see the light. That never failed to make me laugh—
your complacent assumption that like the Prodigal of
His fairy tale, I——

FATHER BAIRD (*sharply*). Jack! You promised!

JOHN (*confusedly*). I know. I didn't mean—— Go
on with what you started to tell me.

FATHER BAIRD. First answer me frankly one question.
Have you been greatly troubled in spirit by anything
lately?

JOHN (*startled*). I? Why do you ask that? Of
course not. (*Then evasively.*) Oh, well—yes, maybe,
if you mean business worries.

FATHER BAIRD. Nothing else?

JOHN. No. What could there be?

26

FATHER BAIRD (*unconvinced—looking away*). The reason I asked—— You'll see in what I'm going to tell you. It happened one night while I was praying for you in my church, as I have every day since I left you. A strange feeling of fear took possession of me—a feeling you were unhappy, in some great spiritual danger. I told myself it was foolish. I'd had a letter from you only that day, reiterating how happy you were. I tried to lose my dread in prayer—and my guilt. Yes, I felt stricken with guilt, too—that I was to blame for whatever was happening to you. Then, as I prayed, suddenly as if by some will outside me, my eyes were drawn to the Cross, to the face of Our Blessed Lord. And it was like a miracle ! His face seemed alive as a living man's would be, but radiant with eternal life, too, especially the sad, pitying eyes. But there was a sternness in His eyes, too, an accusation against me—a command about you ! (*He breaks off and gives John a quick glance, as if afraid of finding him sneering. Then, looking away, he adds simply:*) That's the real reason I decided to take my vacation in the East, Jack.

JOHN (*stares at him fascinatedly*). You saw—— ?

LOVING (*in a bitter, sneering tone*). It could hardly have been any concern for me you saw in His face—even if He did exist or ever had existed !

FATHER BAIRD (*sternly*). Jack ! (*Then, after a pause, quietly.*) Do you know Francis Thompson's poem—The Hound of Heaven ?

LOVING. I did once. Why ?

FATHER BAIRD (*quotes in a low voice but with deep feeling*).

27

" Ah, fondest, blindest, weakest,
I am He Whom thou seekest !
Thou dravest love from thee, who dravest Me."

LOVING (*in what is close to a snarl of scorn*).   Love !

JOHN (*defensively*).   I have love !

FATHER BAIRD (*as if he hadn't heard*).   Why do you run and hide from Him, as from an enemy ?   Take care. There comes a time in every man's life when he must have his God for friend, or he has no friend at all, not even himself.   Who knows ?   Perhaps you are on the threshold of that time now.

JOHN (*uneasily*).   What do you mean ?

FATHER BAIRD.   I don't know.   It's for you to know that.   You say you have love ?

JOHN.   You know I have.   Or, if you don't, you soon will after you've met Elsa.

FATHER BAIRD.   I'm not doubting your love for her nor hers for you.   It's exactly because I do not doubt. I am thinking that such love needs the hope and promise of eternity to fulfil itself—above all, to feel itself secure. Beyond the love for each other should be the love of God, in Whose Love yours may find the triumph over death.

LOVING (*sneeringly*).   Old superstition, born of fear ! Beyond death there is nothing.   That, at least, is certain —a certainty we should be thankful for.   One life is boring enough.   Do not condemn us to another.   Let us rest in peace at last !

FATHER BAIRD (*quietly*).   Would you talk that way if Elsa should die ?

JOHN (*with a shudder*). For God's sake, don't speak about——

LOVING. Do you think I haven't imagined her death many times?

JOHN. The dread of it has haunted me ever since we were married.

FATHER BAIRD. Ah!

LOVING. You'll see that I face it—by proxy, at least —in my novel. (*A sneering taunt in his voice.*) I think you'll be interested in this novel, Uncle.

FATHER BAIRD (*staring at John, whose face is averted*). It's autobiographical, then?

JOHN (*hastily*). No. Of course not. I only meant—— Don't get that idea in your head, for Pete's sake. As I explained to Elsa, when I told her about the first part, it's really the story of a man I once knew.

LOVING. The first part will particularly interest you, Uncle. I am afraid you will be terribly shocked— especially in the light of your recent mystic vision!

FATHER BAIRD. I'm very curious to hear it, Jack. When will you tell me?

LOVING (*defiantly*). Now!

JOHN (*uneasily*). But no. I don't want to bore you.

FATHER BAIRD. You won't bore me.

JOHN. No—— I——

LOVING (*with harsh insistence*). The first part concerns my hero's boyhood here in New York, up to the age of fifteen.

JOHN (*under Loving's compulsion, he picks up the thread of the story*). He was an only child. His father was a fine man. The boy adored him. And he adored his mother even more. She was a wonderful woman, a perfect type of our old beautiful ideal of wife and mother.

LOVING (*sneeringly*). But there was one ridiculous weakness in her character, an absurd obsession with religion. In the father's, too. They were both devout Catholics.

> (*The priest gives a swift, reproachful look at John, seems about to protest, thinks better of it, and drops his eyes.*)

JOHN (*quickly*). But not the ignorant, bigoted sort, please understand. No, their piety had a genuine, gentle, mystic quality to it. Their faith was the great comforting inspiration of their lives. And their God was One of Infinite Love—not a stern, self-righteous Being Who condemned sinners to torment, but a very human, lovable God Who became man for love of men and gave His life that they might be saved from themselves. And the boy had every reason to believe in such a Divinity of Love as the Creator of Life. His home atmosphere was one of love. Life *was* love for him then. And he was happy, happier than he ever afterward—— (*He checks himself abruptly.*)

FATHER BAIRD (*nods his head approvingly*). Yes.

JOHN. Later, at school, he learned of the God of Punishment, and he wondered. He couldn't reconcile Him with his parents' faith. So it didn't make much impression on him.

LOVING (*bitterly*). Then ! But afterward he had good reason to——

30

JOHN. But then he was too sure in his faith. He grew up as devout as his parents. He even dreamed of becoming a priest. He used to love to kneel in the church before the Cross.

LOVING. Oh, he was a remarkably superstitious young fool ! (*His voice suddenly changes to hard bitterness.*) And then when he was fifteen all these pious illusions of his were destroyed for ever ! Both his parents were killed !

JOHN (*hurriedly*). That is, they died during a flu epidemic in which they contracted pneumonia—and he was left alone—without love. First, his father died. The boy had prayed with perfect faith that his father's life might be spared.

LOVING. But his father died ! And the poor simpleton's naïve faith was a bit shaken, and a sinful doubt concerning the Divine Love assailed him !

JOHN. Then his mother, worn out by nursing his father and by her grief, was taken ill. And the horrible fear came to him that she might die, too.

LOVING. It drove the young idiot into a panic of superstitious remorse. He imagined her sickness was a terrible warning to him, a punishment for the doubt inspired in him by his father's death. (*With harsh bitterness.*) His God of Love was beginning to show Himself as a God of Vengeance, you see !

JOHN. But he still trusted in His Love. Surely He would not take his mother from him, too.

LOVING. So the poor fool prayed and prayed and vowed his life to piety and good works ! But he began to make a condition now——*if* his mother were spared to him !

JOHN.   Finally he knew in his heart she was going to die.   But even then he hoped and prayed for a miracle.

LOVING.   He abased and humbled himself before the Cross——and, in reward for his sickening humiliation, saw that no miracle would happen.

JOHN.   Something snapped in him then.

LOVING (*his voice suddenly takes on a tone of bitter hatred*). He saw his God as deaf and blind and merciless——a Deity Who returned hate for love and revenged Himself upon those who trusted Him !

JOHN.   His mother died.   And, in a frenzy of insane grief——

LOVING.   No !   In his awakened pride he cursed his God and denied Him, and, in revenge, promised his soul to the Devil——on his knees, when everyone thought he was praying !   (*He laughs with malignant bitterness.*)

JOHN (*quickly——in a casual tone*).   And that's the end of Part One, as I've outlined it.

FATHER BAIRD (*horrified*).   Jack !   I can't believe that you——

JOHN (*defensively*).   I ?   What have I to do with it ? You're forgetting I explained to you——   Oh, I admit there are certain points of resemblance between some of his boyhood experiences and mine——his parents' death, for example.   But that's only coincidence.

FATHER BAIRD (*recovered now——staring at him——quietly*). I see.

32

JOHN (*forcing a smile*). And please don't bring up those coincidences before Elsa, Uncle. She didn't notice them because I've never bored her with boyhood reminiscences. And I don't want her to get the wrong angle on my plot.

FATHER BAIRD. I'll remember, Jack. When will you tell me the rest of it?

JOHN. Oh, some time while you're here, maybe.

FATHER BAIRD. Why not to-night at your home?

JOHN. Well, I might——

LOVING. That is, if I can decide on my end before then!

JOHN. It would give me a chance to get your and Elsa's criticisms at the same time. She's been wanting to hear the rest of it, too.

FATHER BAIRD (*regarding him—quietly*). Then, by all means. (*Abruptly changing to a brisk casualness.*) Well, I'll leave you and attend to some errand I have to do. (*He gets to his feet. He takes John's hand.*)

JOHN. Dinner is at seven-thirty. But come as long before that as you like. I'll be home early. (*Then with a genuine boyish affection.*) I want to tell you again, Uncle, how grand it is to have you here—in spite of our arguments.

FATHER BAIRD. I'm not worried by our arguments. But I am about something about you that admits of no argument——to me.

JOHN (*forcing a smile*). You're wasting worry. But what is it?

FATHER BAIRD. You've written me you were happy, and I believed you. But, now I see you, I don't believe you. You're not happy. Why? Perhaps if you had it out with me——

LOVING (*mockingly*). Confess, eh?

JOHN. Don't be foolish, Uncle. I am happy, happier than I ever dreamed I could be. And, for heaven's sake, don't go telling Elsa I'm unhappy!

FATHER BAIRD (*quietly*). Very well. We'll say no more about it. And now I'll be off. Good-bye until this evening, Jack.

JOHN. So long, Uncle.

> (*Father Baird goes out. John stands by the door, looking after him—then he comes slowly back and sits down in his chair and stares before him. Loving's eyes are fastened on him with a cold contempt.*)

LOVING. Damned old fool with his bedtime tales for second childhood about the love of God! And you— you're worse—with your hypocritical lies about your great happiness!

> (*The telephone on the table rings. John jumps nervously—then answers it in an apprehensive voice.*)

JOHN. Hello. Who? Tell her I'm out.

LOVING. You'd better find out what she wants.

JOHN. No, wait, I'll take it. (*Then, his voice becoming guarded and pleasantly casual.*) Hello, Lucy. Bill told me you'd called. What——? (*He listens—then*

34

anxiety creeping into his tone.) She phoned again ? What about ? Oh ! I'm glad you called me. Yes, she has been wondering why she hasn't heard from you in so long. Yes, by all means, go. Yes, she's sure to be in this afternoon. Good-bye. (*He hangs up mechanically.*)

LOVING (*sneeringly*). Your terrible sin begins to close in on you, eh ? But then, it wasn't you, was it ? It was some evil spirit that possessed you ! (*He gives a mocking laugh—then stops abruptly and continues in his tone of cold, sinister insistence.*) But enough of that nonsense. Let's return to your plot. The wife dies—of influenza that turns into pneumonia, let's say.

JOHN (*starts violently—stammers*). What—God damn you—what makes you choose that ?

CURTAIN

ACT TWO

PLOT FOR A NOVEL

(*Continued*)

SCENE. *The living-room of the Lovings' duplex apartment. Venetian blinds soften the light from a big window at right. In front of this window is a table with a lamp. At left, front, an upholstered chair. At right of chair, a small table with a lamp. At right of table, in the centre of the room, a sofa. In front of sofa, a low stand with cigarette-box and ash-trays. Toward right, another chair. In the left wall is a door leading to the dining-room. At rear of door, a writing-desk. In the middle of the rear wall is a doorway leading to the hall.*

It is later the same afternoon.

Elsa enters from the hall at rear. She is thirty-five but looks much younger. She is beautiful with that Indian Summer renewal of physical charm which comes to a woman who loves and is loved, particularly to one who has not found that love until comparatively late in life. This beauty is a trifle dimmed now by traces of recent illness. Her face is drawn and she fights against a depressing lassitude. She wears a simple négligée.

As she comes in, she presses a button by the door and a buzzer is heard in the pantry. She comes forward and sits on the sofa. A moment later Margaret, the maid, appears from the dining-room at left. She is a middle-aged Irishwoman with a kindly face.

MARGARET. Yes, Madame?

ELSA. Hasn't the afternoon paper come yet, Margaret?

MARGARET. No, Madame, not yet. (*Then with kindly reproof.*) Didn't you take a nap like you promised you would?

ELSA. I couldn't get to sleep. But I do feel rested, so don't begin to scold me. (*She smiles and Margaret smiles back, a look of devoted affection lighting up her face.*)

MARGARET. You have to take care. The flu's a bad thing the way it leaves you weak after. And you're only out of your bed two days.

ELSA. Oh, I'm really quite well again. And I was too excited to sleep. I kept thinking of Mr. Loving's uncle.

(*The telephone in the hall rings and Margaret goes toward the door in rear to answer it.*)

Heavens, I hope that isn't he now. Mr. Loving phoned me he told him to come early. But surely he wouldn't this early!

MARGARET (*disappears in the hall. Her voice comes*). Just a moment and I'll see if she's in. (*She appears again in the doorway.*) It's Mrs. Hillman calling to see you, Madame.

ELSA. Oh, I'm glad. Tell her to come right up. (*Margaret disappears and is heard relaying this instruction. Then she appears in the hall outside the doorway, waiting to answer the door. Elsa speaks to her.*) I wish I didn't look so like a sick cat. Why is it everyone decides to turn up when you look your worst ?

MARGARET. Ah, you needn't worry, Madame. You look fine.

ELSA. Well, anyway, I don't mind Lucy.

> (*Nevertheless, she goes to the desk at left, rear, takes out a vanity case, powders her nose, etc. While she is doing this, Margaret moves to the entrance door in the hall and is heard admitting Mrs. Hillman and exchanging greetings with her, as she helps her off with her things. Elsa calls.*)

Hello, Stranger.

LUCY (*calls back in a voice whose breeziness rings a bit strained*). That's right, sit on me the minute I set foot in your house ! Well, I know I deserve it.

> (*Elsa goes to the doorway and meets her as she comes in, kissing her affectionately. Lucy Hillman is about the same age as Elsa. She is still an extremely attractive woman but, in contrast to Elsa, her age shows, in spite of a heavy make-up. There are wrinkles about her eyes, and her small, full, rather weak mouth is drawn down by sharp lines at the corners. She is dressed expensively in clothes a bit too youthful and extreme in style. She responds to Elsa's greeting with a nervous constraint.*)

Hello, Elsa.

ELSA. You're a nice one ! How long has it been

38

—months !—not since before I went to Boston in February. _(She sits on the sofa and draws Lucy down beside her.)_

LUCY. I know. I'm in the dust at your feet.

ELSA. I've phoned you a dozen times, but you were always out. Or did you just tell them to say that? I've completely lost faith in you.

LUCY. But I was out, Elsa. How can you think——

ELSA _(laughing—gives her a hug)_. You're not taking me seriously, are you? I know you'd hardly do that with me, after all these years.

LUCY. Of course, I wouldn't.

ELSA. But I did wonder a little at your sudden complete ignoring of our existence. So did John.

LUCY _(hurriedly)_. If you know all the stupid engagements that pile up—and all the idiotic parties Walter lets me in for. _(Then changing the subject abruptly.)_ May I have a cigarette? _(She takes one from the box on the stand and lights it.)_ Aren't you having one?

ELSA. Not now. _(She gives Lucy a puzzled glance. Lucy avoids her eyes, nervously flipping her cigarette over the ash-tray. Elsa asks:)_ How are the kids?

LUCY. Oh, fine, thanks. At least, I think so, from the little I get to see of them nowadays. _(Bitterness has crept into this last. She again hurriedly changes the subject.)_ But tell me all your news. What have you been doing with yourself?

ELSA. Oh, the same peaceful routine—going to a

39

concert now and then, reading a lot, keeping house, taking care of John.

LUCY. The old perfect marriage that's been the wonder of us all, eh ? (*Again changing the subject.*) What time does John usually get home ? I don't want to run into him.

ELSA. Oh, not for an hour or so yet. (*Smiling.*) But why ? What have you got against John ?

LUCY (*smiling with a strange wryness*). Nothing— except myself. (*Then hurriedly.*) I mean, look at me, I look like hell. I've had the damnedest insomnia lately. And I'm vain enough not to crave any male viewing the wreckage until I've spruced up on a bath and cocktails.

ELSA. But that's silly. You look wonderful.

LUCY (*dryly*). Thanks, liar ! (*With a side glance of frank envy—unable to keep resentment out of her voice.*) I especially don't care to be up for inspection beside you. The contrast is too glaring.

ELSA. But it's I who look like the devil, not you. I'm just getting over flu.

LUCY. Flu makes—no, never mind. It doesn't affect —what I mean. (*Then with a hard flippant air.*) Pardon me if I seem to indulge in the melancholy jitters. I'm becoming the damnedest whiner and self-pitier. It's really too boring.

> (*She lights another cigarette. Her hands have a nervous tremor. Elsa watches her with a worried, affectionately pitying look.*)

ELSA. What is it, Lucy ? Tell me.

LUCY (*stiffening defensively*). What is what?

ELSA. I want to know what's troubling you. Now, there's no use denying it. I've known you too long. I felt it the moment you came in, that you were upset about something and trying to hide it.

LUCY. I don't know where you got that idea. (*Defensively flippant.*) Oh, really now, Elsa. Don't you go psychic on us!

ELSA. All right, then. Forgive my trying to pump u. But you got me into the bad habit yourself, you .now, by always coming to me with your troubles. I only thought I might be able to help.

LUCY. You! (*She gives a hard little laugh.*)

ELSA (*hurt*). You used to think I could.

LUCY. "Once, long ago———" (*Then, suddenly with repentant shamefacedness.*) Forgive me, Elsa. I'm rotten to be flip about that. You've been the most wonderful friend. And I'm such an ungrateful little slut!

ELSA. Lucy! You mustn't say that.

LUCY (*hurries on with a simulation of frankness*). But honestly, you're mistaken this time. There's nothing wrong, except what seems to be wrong with everyone, the stupid lives we lead—and, of course, the usual financial worries. So please don't bother your head about my troubles.

ELSA. All right, dear. (*Then, after a slight pause— casually*). How is Walter these days?

LUCY (*with a twisted smile*). I thought we weren't going to talk about my troubles! Oh, Walter is—

Walter. You know him, Elsa. Why ask? But do you know anyone, I wonder? Darned if I think you ever see what people really are. You somehow manage to live in some lost world where human beings are still decent and honourable. I don't see how you do it. If you'd always been a little innocent, protected from all ugly contacts——. But, my God, your first marriage must have slapped your face with about every filthy thing a man can be—and that's plenty! Yet you sit here, calm and beautiful and unscarred—— !

ELSA (*quietly*). I had my share of scars. But the wounds are all healed—completely healed. John's love has done that for me.

LUCY. Yes—of course. (*Then, as if she couldn't control herself, she bursts out:*) Oh, you and your John! You bring him up as the answer to everything.

ELSA (*smiling*). Well, he is for me.

LUCY. Do you mean to tell me you're as much in love with him now as when you married him?

ELSA. Oh, much more so, for he's become my child and father now, as well as being a husband and——

LUCY. Lover. Say it. How incredibly mid-Victorian you can be! Don't you know that's all we married ladies discuss nowadays? But you're lucky. Usually the men discussed aren't our husbands, and aren't even good lovers. But never say die. We keep on hoping and experimenting!

ELSA (*repelled*). Don't talk in that disgusting way. I know you don't mean a word of it.

LUCY (*stares at her resentfully for a second, then turns*

away, reaching for another cigarette—dryly). Oh, you're quite sure of that, are you ?

ELSA (*gently*). Lucy, what is it has made you so bitter ? I've noticed it growing on you for the past few years, but now it's completely got you. I—honestly, I hardly know you this time, you've changed so.

LUCY (*hurriedly*). Oh, it's nothing that happened lately. You mustn't get that idea. (*Then letting herself go—with increasing bitterness.*) It's simply that I've grown sick of my life, sick of all the lying and faking of it, sick of marriage and motherhood, sick of myself ! Particularly sick of myself because I endure the humiliation of Walter's open affairs with every damned floosie he meets ! And I'm tired of pretending I don't mind, tired of really minding underneath, tired of pretending to myself I have to go on for the children's sakes, and that they make up to me for everything, which they don't at all !

ELSA (*indignantly*). How can Walter be such a beast !

LUCY (*with a look at Elsa that is almost vindictive*). Oh, he's no worse than a lot of others. At least, he doesn't lie about it.

ELSA. But, for heaven's sake, why do you stand it ? Why don't you leave him ?

LUCY. Oh, don't be so superior and scornful, Elsa. I'll bet you wouldn't—— (*She checks herself abruptly.*)

ELSA. What do you mean ? You know very well I left my first husband the minute I found out——

LUCY (*hurriedly*). I know. I didn't—— Why don't I leave Walter ? I guess because I'm too worn out to have the guts. And then I did try it once. The first time I knew he'd been unfaithful I did the correct thing and went home. I intended to tell Father I was through as Walter's wife. Only Father was away. Mother was there, and I broke down and told her. She took it quite philosophically—said I was a fool to expect too much, men were like that, even my father had—— (*She gives a little shiver of aversion.*) That sort of squelched me. So I went back to Walter and he doesn't know to this day I ever left him.

ELSA. I'm so sorry, Lucy.

LUCY (*returning to her air of hard cynicism*). No pity, please. After all, the situation has its compensations. He has tried nobly to be fair. He said I could have equal liberty to indulge any of my sexual whims.

ELSA. What a stupid fool !

LUCY (*bitterly*). Oh, he didn't really mean it, you know. His vanity couldn't admit I'd ever feel the slightest desire outside of him. It was only a silly gesture he felt safe in making because he was so damned sure of me—because he knows, damn him, that in spite of all he's done to kill it there's still a cowardly slavish something in me, dating back to the happiness of our first married days, which still—loves him ! (*She starts to break down, but fights this back and bursts out vindictively, a look of ugly satisfaction coming into her face.*) But I warned him he'd humiliate me once too often—and he did !

ELSA (*shocked*). You mean you——

LUCY (*with a return of her flippant tone*). Yes, I went in for a little fleeting adultery. And I must say, as a love substitute or even a pleasurable diversion, it's greatly overrated. (*She gives a hard little laugh.*) How horribly shocked you look ! Are you going to order me from your virtuous home ?

ELSA. Lucy ! Don't talk like that ! It's only that I can't believe—none of this is really you. That's what makes it so—— But please don't think I'm condemning you. You know how I love you, don't you ?

LUCY (*stares at her with a strange panic*). Don't, for God's sake ! I don't want you to love me ! I'd rather you hated me !

> (*But Elsa pulls her to her and she breaks down finally, sobbing, her face buried against Elsa's shoulder.*)

ELSA. There, there. You mustn't, dear. (*Then as Lucy grows calmer—quietly.*) Don't think I don't understand, because I do. I felt exactly the same when I found out about Ned Howell. Even though I'd stopped caring for him and our marriage had always been unhappy, my pride was so hurt I wanted to revenge myself and take the first man I met for a lover.

LUCY (*looks up in amazement*). You went through that ? I never dreamed——

ELSA. All that saved me from doing something stupid was the faith I had that somewhere the man was waiting whom I could really love. I felt I owed it to him and to my own self-respect not to deliberately disfigure myself out of wounded pride and spite.

LUCY (*with sad bitterness*). You hit it when you say disfigure. That's how I've felt ever since. Cheap ! Ugly ! As if *I'd* deliberately disfigured *myself*. And not only myself—the man—and others I wouldn't hurt for anything in the world—if I was in my right mind. But I wasn't ! You realize I wasn't, don't you, Elsa ? You must ! You above everyone !

ELSA. I do, dear. Of course I do.

LUCY. I've got to tell you just how it came to happen —so you'll see. It was one of Walter's parties. You know the would-be Bohemian gang he likes to have. They were there in all their vulgarity, their poisonous, envious tongues wise-cracking at everything with any decent human dignity and worth. Oh, there were a few others there, too—our own people—this man was one of them. Walter was drunk, pawing over his latest female, and she got him to go home with her. Everybody watched me to see how I'd take it. I wanted to kill him and her, but I only laughed and had some more to drink. But I was in hell, I can tell you, and inside I kept swearing to myself that I'd show Walter—— And I picked out this man—yes, deliberately ! It was all deliberate and crazy ! And I had to do all the seducing —because he's quite happy. I knew that, but I was crazy. His happiness filled me with rage—the thought that he made others happy. I wanted to take his happiness from him and kill it as mine had been killed !

ELSA. Lucy !

LUCY (*with a hard laugh*). I told you I was in hell, didn't I ? You can't live there without becoming like the rest of the crowd ! (*Hurrying on with her story.*) I got him in my bedroom on some excuse. But he pushed me away, as if he were disgusted with himself and me. But I wouldn't let him go. And then came the strange part of it. Suddenly, I don't know how to explain it, you'll think I'm crazy, or being funny, but it was as if he were no longer there. It was another man, a stranger whose eyes were hateful and frightening. He seemed to look through me at someone else, and I seemed for a moment to be watching some hidden place in his mind where there was something as evil and revengeful as I was. It frightened and fascinated me—and called to me too ; that's the hell of it ! (*She forces a laugh.*) I suppose all this sounds too preposterous. Well, maybe it was the booze working. I'd had a lot. (*She reaches for a cigarette—returning to her hard flippancy.*) And then followed my little dip into adultery.

ELSA (*with a little shiver of repulsion*). Oh !

LUCY. But what a hideous bore this must be to you. Why did I have to tell you, I wonder. It was the last thing I ever wanted—— (*Turns on her in a flash of resentful vindictiveness.*) It makes me out worse than you expected, eh ? But suppose John were unfaithful to you——

ELSA (*startled—frightenedly*). Don't ! (*Then indignantly.*) Lucy ! I won't have you say that, not even——

LUCY. I'm only asking you to suppose.

ELSA. I can't ! I won't ! And I won't let you ! It's too—— ! (*Then controlling herself—forcing a smile.*) But I'm a bigger fool than you are to get angry. You simply don't know John, that's all. You don't know what an old-fashioned romantic idealist he is at heart about love and marriage. And I thank God he is ! You'll laugh at me but I know he never had a single affair in his life before he met me.

LUCY. Oh, come on, Elsa. That's too much !

ELSA. Oh, please don't think I'm a naïve fool. I was as cynical about men in those days as you are now. I wouldn't have believed it of another man in the world, but with John I felt it was absolutely true to what I knew he was like inside him.

LUCY. You loved him and you wanted to believe.

ELSA. No. Even before I loved him, I felt that. It was what made me love him, more than anything else —the feeling that he would be mine, only mine, that I wouldn't have to share him even with the past. If you only could realize how much that meant to me—especially at that time, when I was still full of the disgust and hurt of my first marriage.

LUCY. Well, that's all very fine, but it's not proving to me how you can be so certain that never since then——

ELSA (*proudly*). I know he loves me. I know he knows how much I love him. He knows what that would do to me. It would kill for ever all my faith in life— all truth, all beauty, all love ! I wouldn't want to live !

LUCY. You shouldn't let yourself be so completely at the mercy of any man—not even John.

ELSA. I'm not afraid. (*She smiles.*) The trouble with you is, you old cynic, you can't admit that our marriage is a real ideal marriage. But it is—and that's entirely John's work, not mine.

LUCY. His work ?

ELSA. Yes. When I first met him I thought I was through with marriage for good. Even after I fell in love with him, I didn't want to marry. I was afraid of marriage. I proposed quite frankly that we should simply live together and each keep entire freedom of action. (*She laughs.*) Oh, I was quite ultra-modern about it ! And it shocked John terribly, poor dear—in spite of all his old radical ideas. I'm sure it almost disillusioned him with me for life ! He sternly scorned my offer. He argued with me. How he argued—like a missionary converting a heathen ! He said he loathed the ordinary marriage as much as I did, but that the ideal in back of marriage was a beautiful one, and he knew we could realize that ideal.

LUCY. Ah, yes, the ideal ! I heard a little talk about that once, too !

ELSA. He said no matter if every other marriage on earth were rotten and a lie, our love could make ours into a true sacrament—sacrament was the word he used —a sacrament of faith in which each of us would find the completest self-expression in making our union a beautiful thing. (*She smiles lovingly.*) You see, all this was what I had longed to hear the man I loved say about the spiritual depth of his love for me—what every woman dreams of hearing her lover say, I think.

LUCY (*stirring uneasily—mechanically*). Yes. I know.

ELSA. And, of course, it blew my petty modern selfishness right out the window. I couldn't believe he meant it at first, but when I saw he did, that finished me. (*She smiles—then with quiet pride.*) And I think we've lived up to that ideal ever since. I hope I have. I know he has. It was his creation, you see.

LUCY. Of course he has. Of course.

ELSA.   And our marriage has meant for us, not slavery or boredom but freedom and harmony within ourselves —and happiness.   So we must have both lived true to it. Happiness is proof, isn't it ?

LUCY (*deeply moved—without looking at Elsa, takes her hand and squeezes it—huskily*).   Of course it is.   Please forget the stupid rot I've said.   I was only trying to get a rise out of you.   We all know how wonderfully happy you and John are.   Only remember, the world is full of spiteful liars who would do anything to wreck your happiness and drag you down to their level—what I was doing.   So never listen——   But of course you won't, will you ?   You have faith.   (*She turns and kisses her impulsively.*)   God bless you—and preserve your happiness !

ELSA.   Thank you, Lucy.   That's dear of you. (*Then puzzledly.*)   But why should you be afraid that anyone——

LUCY (*jumps to her feet nervously*).   Only my morbidness.   I've been accused of so many rotten things I never did that I suppose I'm hipped on the subject. (*Then abruptly.*)   Got to run now, Elsa—go home and get on my armour for another of Walter's parties.   It's a gay life.   The only hope is he'll be so broke before long no one will call on us but our forgotten friends.   (*She gives a bitter little laugh and starts to go around the left of sofa—then, at a noise of a door opening in the hall—nervously.*)   Isn't that someone—— ?

ELSA.   It must be John.   (*She hurries around the right of sofa and back towards the doorway.*)

JOHN (*calls from the hall*).   Hello.

ELSA (*going out, meets him as he appears in the hall*

just beyond the doorway—kissing him). Hello, darling. You're early. I'm so glad.

JOHN. I thought, as I'd told Uncle to come early, I better—— *(He kisses her.)* How do you feel, dear? You look much better.

ELSA. Oh, I'm fine, John.

> *(Lucy has remained standing by the left corner of the sofa, in a stiff, strained attitude, the expression on her face that of one caught in a corner, steeling herself for an ordeal. Elsa and John come in, their arms around each other. As they do so, Lucy recovers her poise and calls to him.)*

LUCY. Hello, John.

JOHN *(coming to her, his face wearing its most cordial, poker-faced smile).* Why, hello, Lucy, I thought I heard a familiar voice when I came in. *(They shake hands.)* A pleasant surprise. Been a long time since we've had this pleasure.

> *(Elsa has come forward behind him. The figure of the masked Loving appears in the doorway. During the next few speeches he moves silently to the corner of the long table before the window, right-front, and stands there, without looking at them, facing front, his eyes fixed in the same cold stare, the expression of his masked face seeming to be more than ever sneering and sinister.)*

LUCY. Now, don't you begin on that! Elsa has already given me hell.

ELSA (*laughing*). And she's repented and been forgiven.

JOHN. Oh, that's all right, then.

LUCY (*nervously*). I was just leaving. Sorry I've got to run, John.

ELSA. Oh, you can't, now. John will think he's driven you out.

LUCY. No, really, Elsa, I——

ELSA. You simply must keep John company for a few minutes. Because I've got to go to the kitchen. I trust Emmy on ordinary occasions, but when a long-lost uncle is coming to dinner, a little personal supervision is in order. (*She moves toward the dining-room at left.*)

LUCY (*with a note of desperation*). Well—but I can't stay more than a second.

ELSA. I'll be back right away.

> (*She disappears through the dining-room door. The moment she is gone, John's cordial smile vanishes and his face takes on a tense, harried look. He is now standing behind the right end of sofa, Lucy behind the left end. In the pause while they wait for Elsa to get out of earshot, Loving moves silently over until he is standing just behind John but a step toward rear from him, facing half toward him, half toward front.*)

JOHN (*lowering his voice—hurriedly*). I hope you've been careful and not said anything that——

LUCY. Might give you away? Of course, I didn't.

And even if I were rotten enough to come right out and tell her, she'd never believe me, she has such a touching faith in you.

JOHN (*wincing*). Don't !

LUCY. No. You're perfectly safe. There's only one thing I've got to warn you about. It's nothing, really, but——

JOHN. What ?

LUCY. Walter has been telling people. He has to, you see, to keep up his pose of friendly understanding——

JOHN. But how does Walter know ?

LUCY. Don't look so dismayed ! He doesn't know —who it was. And you'd be the last one he'd ever suspect.

JOHN. How is it he knows about you ?

LUCY (*hesitates—then defiantly*). I told him.

JOHN. You told him ? In God's name, why ? But I know. You couldn't resist—watching him squirm !

LUCY (*stung*). Exactly, John. Why do you suppose I ever did it, except for his benefit—if you want the truth.

JOHN. Good God, don't you think I know that ? Do you imagine I ever thought it was anything but revenge on your part ?

LUCY. And whom were you revenging yourself on, John ?—now we're being frank.

LOVING (*with sinister mockery*). Who knows ? Perhaps on love. Perhaps, in my soul, I hate love !

53

LUCY (*stares at John with frightened bewilderment*). John ! Now you're like—that night !

JOHN (*confusedly*). I ? It wasn't I. (*Angrily.*) What do you mean by saying I was revenging myself ? Why should I revenge myself on her ?

LUCY. I don't know, John. That's a matter for your conscience. I've got enough on my own, thank you. I must say I resent your attitude, John. (*With a flippant sneer.*) Hardly the lover-like tone, is it ?

JOHN (*with disgust*). Lover !

LUCY. Oh, I know. I feel the same way. But why hate me ? Why not hate yourself ?

JOHN. As if I didn't ! Good God, if you knew ! (*Then bitterly.*) And how long do you think you'll be able to resist telling Walter it was I, his old friend— so you can watch him squirm some more !

LUCY. John !

JOHN. And Walter will have to tell that to everyone, too—to live up to his pose ! And then——

LUCY. John ! You know I wouldn't, even if I hated you as you seem to hate me. I wouldn't for Elsa's sake. Oh, I know you think I'm a rotten liar, but I love Elsa ! (*Then brokenly.*) Oh, it's such a vile mess ! What fools we were !

JOHN (*dully*). Yes. (*Bitterly again.*) I'm sorry I can't trust you, Lucy. I can when you're yourself. But full of booze—— I see what it will come to. I'll have to tell her myself to save her the humiliation of hearing it through dirty gossip !

LUCY. John ! Oh, please don't be such a fool ! Please !

JOHN. You think she couldn't forgive ?

LUCY. I'm thinking of what it would do to her. Can't you see—— ?

JOHN (*warningly, as he hears the pantry door opening*). Ssshh ! (*Quickly, raising his voice to a conversational tone.*) Uncle is a grand old fellow. You'll have to meet him some time. You'd like him.

LUCY. I'm sure I would. (*Then, as Elsa comes in from the dining-room.*) Ah, here you are. Well, I've got to fly. (*She holds out her hand to John.*) Good-bye, John. Take care of Elsa.

JOHN. Good-bye, Lucy.

> (*Elsa puts an arm around her waist and they go back to the hall doorway.*)

ELSA. I'll get your things.

> (*They disappear in the hall. As soon as they have gone, John turns and, coming around the sofa, sits down on it and stares before him with hunted eyes. Loving moves until he is standing directly behind him. He bends over and whispers mockingly.*)

LOVING. I warned you it was closing in ! You had better make up your mind now to tell the rest of your novel to-night—while there is still time !

JOHN (*tensely*). Yes. I must.

LOVING. But, first it still remains to decide what is to

be your hero's end. (*He gives a little jeering laugh.*) Strange, isn't it, what difficult problems your little dabble in fiction has brought up which demand a final answer !

> (*He laughs again—then turns to face the doorway as Elsa re-enters the room. His eyes remain fixed on her as she comes forward. She comes quietly to the right end of the sofa. John does not notice her coming. Loving remains standing at right, rear, of John.*)

ELSA. A penny for your thoughts, John. (*He starts. She sits down beside him—with a smile.*) Did I scare you ?

JOHN (*forcing a smile*). Don't know what's the matter with me. I seem to have the nervous jumps lately. (*Then carelessly.*) Glad to see Lucy again, were you ?

ELSA. Yes—of course. Only she's changed so. Poor Lucy.

JOHN. Why poor ? Oh, you mean on account of Walter's antics ?

ELSA. Then you know ?

JOHN. Who doesn't ? He's been making as public an ass of himself as possible. But let's not talk about Walter. What did you think of the big event to-day : Uncle dropping out of the blue ?

ELSA. It must have been a surprise for you. I'm dying to meet him. I'm so glad he could come to-night.

JOHN. Yes. So am I.

> (*As if his conversation had run dry, he falls into an uneasy silence. Elsa looks at him worriedly. Then she nestles up close to him.*)

56

ELSA (*tenderly*).   Still love me, do you?

JOHN (*takes her in his arms and kisses her—with intense feeling*).   You know I do!   There's nothing in life I give a damn about except your love!   You know that, don't you?

ELSA.   Yes, dear.

JOHN (*avoiding her eyes now*).   And you'll always love me—no matter what an unworthy fool I am?

ELSA.   Ssshh!   You mustn't say things like that. It's not true.   (*Then smiling teasingly.*)   Well, if you love me so much, prove it by telling me.

JOHN (*controlling a start*).   Telling you what?

ELSA.   Now, don't pretend.   I know there's something that's been troubling you for weeks—ever since I came back from Boston.

JOHN.   No, honestly, Elsa.

ELSA.   Something you're keeping back because you're afraid of worrying me.   So you might as well confess.

JOHN (*forcing a smile*).   Confess?   And will you promise—to forgive?

ELSA.   Forgive you for not wanting to worry me? Foolish one!

JOHN (*hurriedly*).   No, I was only joking.   There's nothing.

ELSA.   Now!   But I think I can guess.   It's about business, isn't it?

JOHN (*grasps at this*). Well—yes, if you must know.

ELSA. And you were afraid that would upset me? Oh, John, you're such a child at times you ought to be spanked. You must think I've become a poor, helpless doll!

JOHN. No, but——

ELSA. Just because you've pampered me so terribly the past few years! But remember, we had barely enough to get along on when we were married—and I didn't appear so terribly unhappy then, did I? And no matter how poor we become, do you think it would ever really matter one bit to me as long as I had you?

JOHN (*stammers miserably*). Sweetheart! You make me feel—so damned ashamed! God, I can't tell you!

ELSA (*kissing him*). But, darling, it's nothing! And now promise me you'll forget it and not worry any more?

JOHN. Yes.

ELSA. Good! Let's talk of something else. Tell me, have you been doing anything more on the rest of your idea for a novel?

JOHN. Yes, I—I've got most of it thought out.

ELSA (*encouragingly*). That's splendid. You just put your mind on that and forget your silly worries. But when am I going to hear it?

JOHN. Well, I told Uncle the first part and he was curious, too. So I threatened him I might give you both an outline of the rest to-night.

ELSA. Oh, that's fine. (*Then she laughs.*) And I'll confess it will be a great aid to me as a hostess. I'll probably feel a bit self-conscious, entertaining a strange priest-uncle for the first time.

JOHN. Oh, you won't be with him a minute before you'll feel he's an old friend.

ELSA. Well, that sounds encouraging. But you tell your story just the same. (*She gets up.*) It must be getting on. I'd better go up and start getting dressed. (*She goes around the left end of the sofa and back toward the hall door.*) Are you going up to your study for a while?

JOHN. Yes, in a minute. I want to do a little more work on my plot. The end isn't clearly worked out yet.

LOVING. That is, my hero's end!

ELSA (*smiling at John encouragingly*). Then you get busy, by all means, so you'll have no excuse!

(*She goes out. As soon as she is gone, John's expression changes and becomes tense and hunted again. Loving remains standing behind him, staring down at him with cold, scornful eyes. There is a pause of silence.*)

JOHN (*suddenly—his face full of the bitterest, tortured self-loathing—aloud to himself*). You God-damned rotten swine!

LOVING (*mockingly*). Yes, unfit to live. Quite unfit for life, I think. But there is always death to wash one's sins away—sleep, untroubled by Love's betraying dream!

59

(*He gives a low, sinister laugh.*) Merely a consoling reminder—in case you've forgotten !

> (*John listens fascinatedly, as if to an inner voice. Then a look of terror comes into his face and he shudders.*)

JOHN (*torturedly*).   For God's sake !   Leave me alone !

CURTAIN

ACT THREE

PLOT FOR A NOVEL
(*Continued*)

SCENE. *The living-room again. It is immediately after dinner. Father Baird is sitting in the chair at left, front, Elsa on the sofa, John beside her on her left, the masked Loving at right, rear, of John, in the chair by the end of the table before the window. John and Loving are in dinner clothes of identical cut. Elsa wears a white evening gown of extremely simple lines. Father Baird is the same as in Act One.*

Margaret is serving them the after-dinner coffee. She goes out through the dining-room door.

JOHN (*puts an arm around Elsa's waist playfully*). Well, now you've got to know her, what do you think of her, Uncle ? Weren't my letters right ?

FATHER BAIRD (*gallantly*). They were much too feeble. You didn't do her justice by half !

ELSA. Thank you, Father. It's so kind of you to say that.

JOHN. Ah ! I told you that was one subject we'd agree on ! (*Then to Elsa in a tenderly chiding tone.*) But I've got a bone to pick with you, my lady. You ate hardly any dinner, do you know it ?

ELSA. Oh, but I did, dear.

JOHN. No, you only went through the motions. I was watching you. That's no way to get back your strength.

FATHER BAIRD. Yes, you need all the nourishment you can take when you're getting over the flu.

JOHN (*worriedly—grasping her hand*). Sure you're warm enough ? Want me to get you something to put over your shoulders ?

ELSA. No, dear, thank you.

JOHN. Remember it's a rotten, chilly, rainy day out and even indoors you can't be too careful.

ELSA. Oh, but I'm quite all right now, John. Please don't worry about me.

JOHN. Well, don't let yourself get tired now, you hear ? If you find yourself feeling at all worn-out, you just send Uncle and me off to my study. He'll understand. Won't you, Uncle ?

FATHER BAIRD. Of course. I hope Elsa will feel I'm one of the family and treat me without ceremony.

ELSA. I do feel that, Father. (*Then teasingly.*) But do you know what I think is behind all this solicitude of John's ? He's simply looking for an excuse to get out of telling us the rest of his novel. But we won't let him back out, will we ?

FATHER BAIRD. Indeed we won't.

ELSA. The first part is so unusual and interesting. Don't you think so, Father ?

FATHER BAIRD (*quietly*). Yes. Tragic and revealing to me.

ELSA. You see, John, it's no use. We're simply going to insist.

LOVING (*coldly mocking*). You're sure—you insist?

ELSA. Of course I do. So come on.

JOHN (*nervously*). Well—— (*He hesitates—gulps down the rest of his coffee.*)

ELSA (*smiling*). I never saw you so flustered before, John. You'd think you were going to address an audience of literary critics.

JOHN (*begins jerkily*). Well—— But before I start, there's one thing I want to impress on you both again. My plot, up to the last part, which is wholly imaginary, is taken from life. It's the story of a man I once knew.

LOVING (*mockingly*). Or thought I. knew.

ELSA. May I be inquisitive? Did I ever know the man?

LOVING (*a hostile, repellent note in his voice*). No. I can swear to that. You have never known him.

ELSA (*taken aback, gives John a wondering look—then apologetically*). I'm sorry I butted in with a silly question. Go on, dear.

JOHN (*nervously—forcing a laugh*). I—— It's hard getting started. (*He turns and reaches for his coffee, forgetting he has drunk it—sets the cup down again abruptly and goes on hurriedly.*) Well, you will remember my first part ended when the boy's parents had died.

LOVING.   And he had denied all his old superstitions !

JOHN.   Well, as you can imagine, for a long while after their deaths, he went through a terrific inner conflict.   He was seized by fits of terror, in which he felt he really had given his soul to some evil power.   He would feel a tortured longing to pray and beg for forgiveness.   It seemed to him that he had forsworn all love for ever—and was cursed.   At these times he wanted only to die.   Once he even took his father's revolver——

LOVING (*sneeringly*).   But he was afraid to face death. He was still too religious-minded, you see, to accept the one beautiful, comforting truth of life : that death is final release, the warm, dark peace of annihilation.

FATHER BAIRD (*quietly*).   I cannot see the beauty and comfort.

LOVING.   He often regretted afterwards he had not had the courage to die then.   It would have saved him so much silly romantic pursuit of meaningless illusions.

ELSA (*uneasily*).   Oh, you mustn't talk that way, John.   It sounds so bitter—and false—coming from you.

JOHN (*confusedly*).   I—— I didn't—— You forget I'm simply following what this man told me.   (*Hurrying on.*)   Well, finally, he came out of this period of black despair.   He taught himself to take a rationalistic attitude.   He read all sorts of scientific books.   He ended up by becoming an atheist.   But his experience had left an indelible scar on his spirit.   There always remained something in him that felt itself damned by life, damned with distrust, cursed with the inability ever to reach a lasting belief in any faith, damned by a fear of the lie hiding behind the mask of truth.

FATHER BAIRD. Ah !

LOVING (*sneeringly*). So romantic, you see—to think of himself as possessed by a damned soul !

JOHN. And in after years, even at the height of his rationalism, he never could explain away a horror of death—and a strange fascination it had for him. And coupled with this was a dread of life—as if he constantly sensed a malignant Spirit hiding behind life, waiting to catch men at its mercy, in their hour of secure happiness—— Something that hated life !—— Something that laughed with mocking scorn !

> (*He stares before him with a fascinated dread, as if he saw this Something before him. Then, suddenly, as if in reply, Loving gives a little mocking laugh, barely audible. John shudders. Elsa and Father Baird start and stare at John uneasily, but he is looking straight ahead and they turn away again.*)

LOVING. A credulous, religious-minded fool, as I've pointed out ! And he carried his credulity into the next period of his life, where he believed in one social or philosophical Ism after another, always on the trail of Truth ! He was never courageous enough to face what he really knew was true, that there is no truth for men, that human life is unimportant and meaningless. No. He was always grasping at some absurd new faith to find an excuse for going on !

JOHN (*proudly*). And he did go on ! And he found his truth at last—in love, where he least expected he ever would find it. For he had always been afraid of love. And when he met the woman who afterwards became his wife and realized he was in love with her, it threw him into a panic of fear. He wanted to run away from her —but found he couldn't.

LOVING (*scornfully*). So he weakly surrendered—and immediately began building a new superstition of love around her.

JOHN. He was happy again for the first time since his parents' death—to his bewildered joy.

LOVING (*mockingly*). And secret fear !

ELSA (*gives John a curious, uneasy glance*). Secret fear ?

JOHN. Yes, he—he came to be afraid of his happiness. His love made him feel at the mercy of that mocking Something he dreaded. And the more peace and security he found in his wife's love, the more he was haunted by fits of horrible foreboding—the recurrent dread that she might die and he would be left alone again, without love. So great was the force of this obsession at times that he felt caught in a trap, desperate——

LOVING. And he often found himself regretting——

JOHN (*hastily*). Against his will——

LOVING (*inexorably*). That he had again let love put him at the mercy of life !

JOHN (*hurriedly*). But, of course, he realized this was all morbid and ridiculous—for wasn't he happier than he had ever dreamed he could be again ?

66

LOVING (*with gloating mockery*). And so he deliberately destroyed that happiness !

ELSA (*startledly*). Destroyed his happiness ? How, John ?

JOHN (*turns to her, forcing a smile*). I'm afraid you will find this part of his story hard to believe, Elsa. This damned fool, who loved his wife more than anything else in life, was unfaithful to her. (*Father Baird starts and stares at him with a shocked expression.*)

ELSA (*frightenedly*). It is—hard to believe. But this part is all the story of the man you knew, isn't it ?

JOHN. Yes, of course, and you mustn't condemn him entirely until you've heard how it came to happen. (*He turns away from her again—jerkily.*) His wife had gone away. It was the first time. He felt lost without her—fearful, disintegrated. His familiar dread seized him. He began imagining all sorts of catastrophes. Horrible pictures formed in his mind. She was run over by a car. Or she had caught pneumonia and lay dying. Every day these evil visions possessed him. He tried to escape them in work. He couldn't. (*He pauses for a second, nerving himself to go on. Then starts again.*) Then one night an old friend called—to drag him off to a party. He loathed such affairs usually, but this time he thought it would help him to escape himself for a while. So he went. He observed with disgust how his friend, who was drunk, was pawing over some woman right under the nose of his wife. He knew that this friend was continually having affairs of this sort and that his wife was aware of it. He had often wondered if she cared, and he was curious now to watch her reactions. And very soon he had an example of what her pride had to endure, for the husband went off openly with his lady. The man felt a great sympathy for her—and, as if she guessed his thought, she came to him, and he overdid himself in being kind. (*He gives a short bitter laugh*.) A great mistake! For she reacted to it in a way that at first shocked him but ended up in arousing his curiosity. He had known her for years. It wasn't like her. It fascinated him, in a way, that she should have become so corrupted. He became interested to see how far she would go with it—purely as an observer, he thought—the poor idiot! (*He laughs again. Father Baird has remained motionless, his eyes on the floor. Elsa's face is pale and set, her eyes have a bewildered, stricken look. John goes on*.) Remember, all this time he saw through her; he laughed to himself at her crude vamping; he felt he was only playing a game. Just as he knew she was playing a game; that it was no desire for him but hatred for her husband that inspired her. (*He gives a short contemptuous laugh again*.) Oh, he had it all analysed quite correctly, considering the known elements. It was the unknown——

FATHER BAIRD (*without raising his head*). Yes.

> (*He casts a quick glance at Elsa, then looks as quickly away. Her eyes are fastened on the floor now. Her face has frozen into a mask with the tense effort she is making not to give herself away*.)

JOHN. He had not the slightest desire for this woman. When she threw herself into his arms, he was repelled. He determined to end the game. He thought of his wife—— (*He forces a laugh*.) But, as I've said, there was the unknown to reckon with. At the thought of his

68

wife, suddenly it was as if something outside him, a hidden spirit of evil, took possession of him.

LOVING (*coldly vindictive now*).   That is, he saw clearly that this situation was the climax of a long death struggle between his wife and him.   The woman with him counted only as a means.   He saw that underneath all his hypocritical pretences he really hated love.   He wanted to deliver himself from its power and be free again. He wanted to kill it !

ELSA (*with horrified pain*).   Oh !   (*Trying to control herself.*)   I—I don't understand.   He hated love ?   He wanted to kill it ?   But that's—too horrible !

JOHN (*stammers confusedly*).   No—I——   Don't you see it wasn't he ?

LOVING.   But, I'm afraid, Elsa, that my hero's silly idea that he was possessed by a demon must strike you as an incredible superstitious excuse to lie out of his responsibility.

FATHER BAIRD (*without lifting his eyes—quietly*).   Quite credible to me, Jack.   One may not give one's soul to a devil of hate—and remain for ever scatheless.

LOVING (*sneeringly*).   As for the adultery itself, the truth is that this poor fool was making a great fuss about nothing—an act as meaningless as that of one fly with another, of equal importance to life !

ELSA (*stares at John as if he had become a stranger—a look of sick repulsion coming over her face*).   John !   You're disgusting !   (*She shrinks away from him to the end of the sofa near Father Baird.*)

JOHN (*stammers confusedly*).   But I—I didn't mean—

69

forgive me. I only said that—as a joke—to get a rise out of Uncle.

FATHER BAIRD (*gives a quick anxious look at Elsa—then quietly, an undercurrent of sternness in his voice*). I don't think it's a joke. But go on with your story, Jack.

JOHN (*forcing himself to go on*). Well I—I know you can imagine the hell he went through from the moment he came to himself and realized the vileness he had been guilty of. He couldn't forgive himself—and that's what his whole being now cried out for—forgiveness !

FATHER BAIRD (*quietly*). I can well believe that, Jack.

JOHN. He wanted to tell his wife and beg for forgiveness—but he was afraid of losing her love. (*He gives a quick glance at Elsa, as if to catch her reaction to this, but she is staring straight before her with a still, set face. He forces a smile and adopts a joking tone.*) And here's where I'd like to have your opinion, Elsa. The question doesn't come up in my story, as you'll see, but—— Could his wife have forgiven him, do you think ?

ELSA (*starts—then tensely*). You want me to put myself in the wife's place ?

JOHN. Yes. I want to see whether the man was a fool or not—in his fear.

ELSA (*after a second's pause—tensely*). No. She could never forgive him.

JOHN (*desperately*). But it wasn't he ! Can't you see——

ELSA. No. I'm afraid—I can't see.

70

JOHN (*dully now*).   Yes.   That's what I thought you'd say.

ELSA.   But what does it matter what I think ?   You said the question of her forgiving doesn't come up in your novel.

LOVING (*coldly*).   Not while the wife is alive.

JOHN (*dully*).   He never tells her.

LOVING.   She becomes seriously ill.

ELSA (*with a start*).   Oh.

LOVING (*in a cold voice, as if he were pronouncing a death sentence*).   'Flu, which turns into pneumonia.   And she dies.

ELSA (*frightenedly now*).   Dies ?

LOVING.   Yes.   I need her death for my end.   (*Then in a sinister, jeering tone.*)   That is, to make my romantic hero come finally to a rational conclusion about his life !

ELSA (*stares before her, not seeming to have heard this last —her eyes full of a strange, horrified fascination—as if she were talking aloud to herself*).   So she dies.

FATHER BAIRD (*after a worried glance at her—an undercurrent of warning in his quiet tone*).   I think you've tired Elsa out with your sensational imaginings, Jack.   I'd spare her, for the present, at least, the fog of gloom your novel is plunging into.

ELSA (*grasps at this—tensely*).   Yes, I'm afraid it has been too exciting——   I really don't feel up to——   During dinner I began to get a headache and it's splitting now.

JOHN (*gets up—worriedly*). But why didn't you tell me? If I'd known that, I'd never have bored you with my damned plot.

ELSA. I—I think I'll lie down here on the sofa—and take some aspirin—and rest for a while. You can go with your uncle up to your study—and tell him the rest of your story there.

FATHER BAIRD (*gets up*). An excellent idea. Come on, Jack, and give your poor wife a respite from the horrors of authorship. (*He goes to the doorway in rear.*)

JOHN (*comes to Elsa. As he does so, Loving comes and stands behind her, at rear of sofa*). I'm so darned sorry, Elsa, if I've——

ELSA. Oh, please! It's only a headache.

JOHN. You—you don't feel really sick, do you, dearest? (*He puts a hand to her forehead timidly.*)

ELSA (*shrinks from his touch*). No, no, it's nothing.

LOVING (*slowly, in his cold tone with its undercurrent of sinister hidden meaning*). You must be very careful, Elsa. Remember it's cold and raining out.

ELSA (*staring before her strangely—repeats fascinatedly*). It's raining?

LOVING. Yes.

JOHN (*stammers confusedly*). Yes, you—you must be careful, dearest.

FATHER BAIRD (*from the doorway in rear—sharply*). Come along, Jack!

*(John goes back to him and Loving follows John.
Father Baird goes into the hall, turning left to go
upstairs to the study. John stops in the doorway and looks back for a moment at Elsa
frightenedly. Loving comes to his side and
also stops and looks at her, his eyes cold and
remorseless in his mask of sinister mockery.
They stand there for a moment side by side.
Then John turns and disappears in the hall
toward left, following Father Baird. Loving
remains, his gaze concentrated on the back of
Elsa's head with a cruel, implacable intensity.
She is still staring before her with the same
strange fascinated dread. Then, as if in
obedience to his will, she rises slowly to her
feet and walks slowly and woodenly back past
him and disappears in the hall, turning right
toward the entrance door to the apartment.
For a second Loving remains looking after her.
Then he turns and disappears in the hall
toward left, following Father Baird and John
to the study.)*

CURTAIN

SCENE TWO

SCENE. *John Loving's study on the upper floor of the apartment. At left, front, is a door leading into Elsa's
bedroom. Bookcases extend along the rear and right
walls. There is a door to the upper hall at rear,
right. A long table with a lamp is at centre, front.
At left of table is a chair. In front of table a similar
chair. At right, front, is a chaise-longue, facing left.*

73

Father Baird, John and Loving are discovered. The priest is sitting on the chaise-longue, John in the chair at front of table, Loving in the chair at left of table. Father Baird sits in the same attitude as he had in the previous scene, his eyes on the floor, his expression sad and a bit stern. Loving's masked face stares at John, his eyes cold and still. John is talking in a strained tone, monotonously, insistently. It is as if he were determinedly talking to keep himself from thinking.

JOHN. I listen to people talking about this universal breakdown we are in and I marvel at their stupid cowardice. It is so obvious that they deliberately cheat themselves because their fear of change won't let them face the truth. They don't want to understand what has happened to them. All they want is to start the merry-go-round of blind greed all over again. They no longer know what they want this country to be, what they want it to become, where they want it to go. It has lost all meaning for them except as a pig-wallow. And so their lives as citizens have no beginnings, no ends. They have lost the ideal of the Land of the Free. Freedom demands initiative, courage, the need to decide what life must mean to oneself. To them, that is terror. They explain away their spiritual cowardice by whining that the time for individualism is past, when it is their courage to possess their own souls which is dead—and stinking ! No, they don't want to be free. Slavery means security—of a kind, the only kind they have courage for. It means they need not think. They have only to obey orders from owners who are, in turn, their slaves !

LOVING (*breaks in—with bored scorn*). But I'm denouncing from my old soap-box again. It's all silly

74

twaddle, of course. Freedom was merely our romantic delusion. We know better now. We know we are all the slaves of meaningless chance—electricity or something, which whirls us—on to Hercules !

JOHN (*with a proud assertiveness*). But, in spite of that, I say : Very well ! On to Hercules ! Let us face that ! Once we have accepted it without evasion, we can begin to create new goals for ourselves, ends for our days ! A new discipline for life will spring into being, a new will and power to live, a new ideal to measure the value of our lives by !

LOVING (*mockingly*). What ? Am I drooling on about my old social ideals again ? Sorry to bore you, Uncle.

FATHER BAIRD (*quietly, without looking up*). You are not boring me, Jack.

JOHN (*an idealistic exaltation coming into his voice*). We need a new leader who will teach us that ideal, who by his life will exemplify it and make it a living truth for us—a man who will prove that man's fleeting life in time and space can be noble. We need, above all, to learn again to believe in the possibility of nobility of spirit in ourselves ! A new saviour must be born who will reveal to us how we can be saved from ourselves, so that we can be free of the past and inherit the future and not perish by it !

LOVING (*mockingly*). Must sound like my old letters to you, Uncle. It's more nonsense, of course. But there are times of stress and flight when one hides in any old empty barrel !

FATHER BAIRD (*ignoring this—quietly*). You are for-

75

getting that men have such a Saviour, Jack. All they need is to remember Him.

JOHN (*slowly*). Yes, perhaps if we could again have faith in——

LOVING (*harshly*). No! We have passed beyond gods! There can be no going back!

FATHER BAIRD. Jack! Take care!

LOVING (*mockingly again*). But, on the other hand, I'll grant you the pseudo-Nietzschean saviour I just evoked out of my past is an equally futile ghost. Even if he came, we'd only send him to the insane asylum for teaching that we should have a nobler aim for our lives than getting all four feet in a trough of swill! (*He laughs sardonically.*) How could we consider such an unpatriotic idea as anything but insane, eh?

(*There is a pause. Father Baird looks up and studies John's face searchingly, hopefully.*)

FATHER BAIRD (*finally speaks quietly*). Jack, ever since we came upstairs, I've listened patiently while you've discussed every subject under the sun except the one I know is really on your mind.

JOHN. I don't know what you mean.

FATHER BAIRD. The end of our story.

JOHN. Oh, forget that. I'm sick of the damned thing—now, at any rate.

FATHER BAIRD. Sick of the damned thing, yes. That's why I feel it's important you tell it—now. This man's wife dies, you said. (*He stares fixedly at John now*

76

and adds slowly.) Of influenza which turns into pneumonia.

JOHN (*uneasily*). Why do you stare like that?

FATHER BAIRD (*dropping his eyes—quietly*). Go on with your story.

JOHN (*hesitantly*). Well—I—— You can imagine the anguish he feels after his wife's death—the guilt which tortures him a thousandfold now she is dead.

FATHER BAIRD. I can well imagine it, Jack.

LOVING (*sneeringly*). And under the influence of his ridiculous guilty conscience, all the superstitions of his childhood, which he had prided himself his reason had killed, return to plague him. He feels at times an absurd impulse to pray. He fights this nonsense back. He analyses it rationally. He sees it clearly as a throwback to boyhood experiences. But, in spite of himself, that cowardly something in him he despises as superstition seduces his reason with the old pathetic life of survival after death. He begins to believe his wife is alive in some mythical hereafter!

JOHN (*strangely*). He knows she knows of his sin now. He can hear her promising to forgive if he can only believe again in his old God of Love, and seek her through Him. She will be beside him in spirit in this life, and at his death she will be waiting. Death will not be an end but a new beginning, a reunion with her in which their love will go on for ever within the eternal peace and love of God! (*His voice has taken on a note of intense longing.*)

FATHER BAIRD. Ah, then you do see, Jack! Thank God!

77

JOHN (*as if he hadn't heard*). One night when he is hounded beyond endurance he rushes out—in the hope that if he walks himself into exhaustion he may be able to sleep for a while and forget. (*Strangely, staring before him, as if he were visualizing the scene he is describing.*) Without his knowing how he got there, he finds he has walked in a circle and is standing before the old church, not far from where he now lives, in which he used to pray as a boy.

LOVING (*jeeringly*). And now we come to the great temptation scene, in which he finally confronts his ghosts ! (*With harsh defiance.*) The church challenges him—and he accepts the challenge and goes in !

JOHN. He finds himself kneeling at the foot of the Cross. And he feels he is forgiven, and the old comforting peace and security and joy steal back into his heart ! (*He hesitates, as if reluctant to go on, as if this were the end.*)

FATHER BAIRD (*deeply moved*). And that is your end ? Thank God !

LOVING (*jeeringly*). I'm afraid your rejoicing is a bit premature—for this cowardly giving in to his weakness is not the end ! Even while he is kneeling, there is a mocking rational something in him that laughs with scorn—and at the last moment his will and pride revive in him again ! He sees clearly by the light of reason the degradation of his pitiable surrender to old ghostly comforts—and he rejects them ! (*His voice with surprising suddenness takes on a savage vindictive quality.*) He curses his God again as he had when a boy ! He defies Him finally ! He——— !

FATHER BAIRD (*sternly*). Jack ! Take care !

JOHN (*protests confusedly*). No—that's not right—I——

LOVING (*strangely confused in his turn—hurriedly*). Pardon me, Uncle. Of course, that's wrong—afraid for a moment I let an author's craving for a dramatic moment run away with my sane judgment. Naturally, he could never be so stupid as to curse what he knew didn't exist !

JOHN (*despondently*). No. He realizes he can never believe in his lost faith again. He walks out of the church—without love for ever now—but daring to face his eternal loss and hopelessness, to accept it as his fate and go on with life.

LOVING (*mockingly*). A very, very heroic end, as you see ! But, unfortunately, absolutely meaningless !

FATHER BAIRD. Yes. Meaningless. I'm glad you see that.

JOHN (*rousing a bit—defensively*). No—I take that back—it isn't meaningless. It is man's duty to life to go on !

LOVING (*jeeringly*). The romantic idealist again speaks ! On to Hercules ! What an inspiring slogan ! (*Then a sinister note coming into his voice.*) But there is still another end to my story—the one sensible happy end !

FATHER BAIRD (*as if he hadn't heard this last*). Jack ! Are you so blind you cannot see what your imagining his finding peace in the church reveals about the longing of your own soul—the salvation from yourself it holds out to you ? Why, if you had any honesty, with yourself, you would get down on your knees now and——

LOVING. Rot ! How can you believe such childish superstition !

FATHER BAIRD (*angrily*). Jack ! I've endured all I can of your blasphemous insults to——

JOHN (*confused—hurriedly*). I—I didn't mean—I'm sorry, Uncle. But it's only a story. Don't take it so seriously.

FATHER BAIRD (*has immediately controlled himself— quietly*). Only a story, Jack ? You're sure you still want me to believe that ?

JOHN (*defensively*). Why, what else could you believe ? Do you think I—— ? (*Then in an abrupt, angry tone.*) But that's enough about the damned story. I don't want to talk any more about it !

> (*Father Baird stares at him but keeps silent. John starts to pace up and down with nervous restlessness—then stops abruptly.*)

I—if you'll excuse me—I think I'll go down and see how Elsa is. (*He goes back toward the door. Loving follows him.*) I'll be right back.

FATHER BAIRD (*quietly*). Of course, Jack. Don't bother about me. I'll take a look at your library.

> (*He gets up. John goes out. Loving turns for a moment to Father Baird, his eyes full of a mocking derision. Then he turns and follows John. Father Baird goes to the bookcase at right and runs his eyes over the titles of books. But he only does this mechanically. His mind is preoccupied, his expression sad and troubled. John's voice can be heard from below calling*

"Elsa." *Father Baird starts and listens. Then from Elsa's bedroom John's voice is heard, as he looks for her there. He calls anxiously "Elsa"—then evidently hurries out again, closing the door behind him. Father Baird's face grows more worried. He goes to the doorway in rear and stands listening to a brief conversation from below. A moment later John comes in from rear. He is making a great effort to conceal a feeling of dread. He comes forward. Loving follows silently but stops and remains standing by the bookcase at left of doorway.)*

JOHN. She's—gone out.

FATHER BAIRD. Gone out? But it's still raining, isn't it?

JOHN. Pouring. I—I can't understand. It's a crazy thing for her to do when she's just getting over——

FATHER BAIRD (*with an involuntary start*). Ah!

JOHN. What?

FATHER BAIRD. Nothing.

JOHN (*frightenedly*). I can't imagine——

FATHER BAIRD. How long has she been gone?

JOHN. I don't know. Margaret says she heard someone go out right after we came upstairs.

FATHER BAIRD (*with lowered voice to himself*). My fault, God forgive me. I had a feeling then I shouldn't leave her.

(John sinks down in the chair by the table and waits tensely—then suddenly he bursts out.)

JOHN. I never should have told her the story ! I'm a God-damned fool.

FATHER BAIRD *(sternly)*. You would be more honest with yourself if you said a self-damned fool ! *(Hearing a sound from below.)* There. Isn't that someone now ?

(John stops for a second to listen, then hurries to the door in rear. Loving remains where he is, standing motionlessly by the bookcase.)

JOHN *(calls)*. Is that you, Elsa ?

ELSA *(from downstairs—hurriedly)*. Yes. Don't come down. I'm coming up.

(A moment later she appears in the hallway.)

JOHN. Darling ! I've been so damned worried. *(He starts to take her in his arms.)*

ELSA. Please !

(She wards him off and steps past him into the study. She has taken off her coat and hat downstairs, but the lower part of her skirt and her stockings and shoes are soaking wet. Her face is pinched and drawn and pale, with flushed spots over the cheek-bones, and her eyes are bright and hard. Father Baird stares at her searchingly, his face sad and pitying.)

FATHER BAIRD *(forcing a light tone—as she comes forward)*. Well ! You have given us a scare, my lady.

ELSA *(tensely)*. I'm sorry, Father.

FATHER BAIRD. Your husband was half out of his mind worrying what had happened to you.

> (*She sits in the chair in front of table. John stands at right of her. Loving has gone up and stands by the right end of table, at right, rear, of John. His eyes are fixed on Elsa's face with an eager, sinister intentness.*)

JOHN (*with increasing uneasiness*). Elsa ! You look sick. Do you feel——— ?

FATHER BAIRD. I'll get her some whisky. And you, make her go to bed at once. (*He goes out the door in rear.*)

JOHN (*grabbing her hands*). Your hands are like ice !

ELSA (*pulls them away from him—coldly, without looking at him*). It's chilly out.

JOHN. Look at your shoes ! They're soaked !

ELSA. It doesn't matter, does it ? (*A chill runs through her body.*)

JOHN. You've taken a chill. (*Then forcing a tenderly bullying tone.*) You'll go right to bed, that's what. And no nonsense about it, you hear !

ELSA. Are you trying the bossy tender husband on me, John ? I'm afraid that's no longer effective.

JOHN (*guiltily*). Why do you say that ?

ELSA. Are you determined to act out this farce to the end ?

JOHN. I—I don't know what you mean. What makes you look at me—as if you hated me ?

ELSA (*bitterly*). Hate you? No, I only hate myself for having been such a fool! (*Then with a hard, mocking tone.*) Shall I tell you where I went, and why? But perhaps I'd better put it in the form of a novel plot!

JOHN. I—I don't know what you're driving at.

ELSA. I went out because I thought I'd like to drop in on one of Lucy's parties. But it wasn't exciting—hardly any adultery going on—I had no opportunity—even if I'd been seized by any peculiar impulse of hatred and revenge on you. So I came home. (*She forces a hard, bitter laugh.*) There! Are you satisfied? It's all a lie, of course. I simply went for a walk. But so is your story about the novel a lie.

JOHN (*stunned—stammers*). Elsa, I——

ELSA. For God's sake, John, don't lie to me any more or I—I know, I tell you! Lucy told me all about it this afternoon.

JOHN. She told you? The damned——

ELSA. Oh, she didn't tell me it was you. But she gave me all the sordid details and they were the same as those in your story. So it was you who told on yourself. Rather a joke on you, isn't it? (*She laughs bitterly.*)

JOHN. I—— (*He blurts out miserably.*) Yes—it's true.

ELSA. And it was a fine joke on me, her coming here. You would appreciate it, if you had seen how I sympathized with her, how I excused her to myself and pitied her. And all the while, she was pitying me! She was gloating! She's always envied us our happiness. Our happiness!

JOHN (*writing*).   Don't !

ELSA.   She must have been laughing at me for a fool, sneering to herself about my stupid faith in you.   And you gave her that chance—you !   You made our love a smutty joke for her and everyone like her—you whom I loved so !   And all the time I was loving you, you were only waiting for this chance to kill that love, you were hating me underneath, hating our happiness, hating the ideal of our marriage you had given me, which had become all the beauty and truth of life to me !   (*She springs to her feet—distractedly.*)   Oh, I can't—— I can't !   (*She starts as if to run from the room.*)

JOHN (*grabbing her—imploringly*).   Elsa !   For God's sake !   Didn't my story explain ?   Can't you believe —it wasn't I ?   Can't you forgive ?

ELSA.   No !   I can't forgive !   How can I forgive —when all that time I loved you so, you were wishing in your heart that I would die !

JOHN (*frantically*).   Don't say that !   It's mad !   Elsa ! Good God, how can you think——

ELSA.   What else can I think ?   (*Then wildly.*)   Oh, John, stop talking !   What's the good of talk ?   I only know I hate life !   It's dirty and insulting—and evil ! I want my dream back—or I want to be dead with it ! (*She is shaken again by a wave of uncontrollable chill, her teeth chatter—pitiably.*)   Oh, John, leave me alone ! I'm cold, I'm sick.   I feel crazy !

FATHER BAIRD (*comes in through the doorway at rear— sharply*).   Jack !   Why haven't you got her to bed ? Can't you see she's ill ?   Phone for your doctor.

(*John goes out. Loving, his eyes remaining fixed on Elsa with the same strange look, backs out of the doorway after him.*)

(*Coming to Elsa—with great compassion.*) My dear child, I can't tell you how deeply——

ELSA (*tensely*). Don't! I can't bear—— (*She is shaken again by a chill.*)

FATHER BAIRD (*worriedly, but trying to pretend to treat it lightly, reassuringly*). You've taken a bad chill. You were very foolhardy to—— But a day or two in bed and you'll be fine again.

ELSA (*strangely serious and bitterly mocking at the same time*). But that would spoil John's story, don't you think? That would be very inconsiderate after he's worked out such a convenient end for me.

FATHER BAIRD. Elsa! For the love of God, don't tell me you took his morbid nonsense seriously! Is that why you——?

ELSA (*as if she hadn't heard him*). And when he reminded me it was raining, it all seemed to fit in so perfectly—like the will of God! (*She laughs with hysterical mockery, her eyes shining feverishly.*)

FATHER BAIRD (*sternly—more to break her mood than because he takes her impiety seriously*). Elsa! Stop that mockery! It has no part in you!

ELSA (*confusedly*). I'm sorry. I forgot you were—— (*Then suddenly hectic again.*) But I've never had any God, you see—until I met John. (*She laughs hysterically—then suddenly forces control on herself and gets shakily to her feet.*) I'm sorry. I seem to be talking nonsense. My head has gone woolly. I——

> (*John enters from the hall at rear. As ne comes forward, Loving appears in the doorway behind him.*)

JOHN (*coming to Elsa*). Stillwell says for you to——

ELSA (*distractedly*). No ! (*Then dully.*) I'll go—to my room. (*She sways weakly. John starts toward her.*)

JOHN. Elsa ! Sweetheart !

ELSA. No !

> (*By an effort of will, she overcomes her weakness and walks woodenly into her bedroom and closes the door behind her. John makes a movement as if to follow her.*)

FATHER BAIRD (*sharply*). Leave her alone, Jack.

> (*John sinks down hopelessly on the chaise-longue. Loving stands behind him, his cold eyes fixed with a sinister intensity on the door through which Elsa has just disappeared. Father Baird makes a movement as if he were going to follow Elsa into her room. Then he stops. There is an expression of sorrowful foreboding on his face. He bows his head with a simple dignity and begins to pray silently.*)

LOVING (*his eyes now on John—with a gloating mockery*). She seems to have taken her end in your story very seriously. Let's hope she doesn't carry that too far ! You have enough on your conscience already—without murder ! You couldn't live, I know, if——

JOHN (*shuddering—clutches his head in both hands as if to crush out his thoughts*). For God's sake! (*His eyes turn to the priest. Then their gaze travels to a point in front of Father Baird, and slowly his expression changes to one of fearful, fascinated awe, as if he suddenly sensed a Presence there the priest is praying to. His lips part and words come haltingly, as if they were forced out of him, full of imploring fear.*) Thou wilt not—do that to me again—wilt Thou? Thou wilt not—take love from me again?

LOVING (*jeeringly*). Is it your old demon you are praying to for mercy? Then I hope you hear his laughter! (*Then breaking into a cold, vicious rage.*) You cowardly fool! I tell you there is nothing—nothing!

JOHN (*starts back to himself—stammers with a confused air of relief*). Yes—of course—what's the matter with me? There's nothing—nothing to fear!

CURTAIN

ACT FOUR
THE END OF THE END

SCENE. *The study is shown as in preceding scene, but this
scene also reveals the interior of Elsa's bedroom at left
of study.*

*At right of bedroom, front, is the door between the two
rooms. At rear of this door, in the middle of the wall,
is a dressing table, mirror and chair. In the left wall,
rear, is the door to the bathroom. Before this door
is a screen. At left, front, is the bed, its head against
the left wall. By the head of the bed is a small stand
on which is a reading lamp with a piece of cloth thrown
over it to dim its light. An upholstered chair is beside
the foot of the bed. Another chair is by the head of the
bed at rear. A chaise-longue is at right, front, of the
room.*

It is nearing daybreak of a day about a week later.

*In the bedroom, Elsa lies in the bed, her eyes closed,
her face pallid and wasted. John sits in the chair
toward the foot of the bed, front. He looks on the
verge of complete mental and physical collapse. His
unshaven cheeks are sunken and sallow. His eyes,
bloodshot from sleeplessness, stare from black hollows
with a frozen anguish at Elsa's face.*

*Loving stands by the back of his chair, facing front.
The sinister, mocking character of his mask is accentuated
now, evilly intensified.*

89

*Father Baird is standing by the middle of the bed,
at rear. His face also bears obvious traces of sleepless
strain. He is conferring in whispers with Doctor
Stillwell, who is standing at his right. Both are
watching Elsa with anxious eyes. At rear of Stillwell
on his right, a trained nurse is standing.*

*Stillwell is in his early fifties, tall, with a sharp,
angular face and grey hair. The Nurse is a plump
woman in her late thirties.*

*For a moment after the curtain rises the whispered
pantomime between Stillwell and the priest continues,
the Nurse watching and listening. Then Elsa stirs
restlessly and moans. She speaks without opening her
eyes, hardly above a whisper, in a tone of despairing
bitterness.*

ELSA. John ! How could you ? Our dream ! (*She
moans.*)

JOHN (*in anguish*). Elsa ! Forgive !

LOVING (*in a cold, inexorable tone*). She will never
forgive.

STILLWELL (*frowning, makes a motion to John to be silent*).
Ssshh !

> (*He whispers to Father Baird, his eyes on John.
> The priest nods and comes around the corner of
> the bed toward John. Stillwell sits in the
> chair by the head of the bed, rear, and feels
> Elsa's pulse. The Nurse moves close behind
> him.*)

FATHER BAIRD (*bends over John's chair and speaks in a
low cautioning voice*). Jack. You must be quiet.

JOHN (*his eyes are on Stillwell's face, desperately trying to read some answer there. He calls to him frightenedly*). Doctor ! What is it ? Is she——— ?

STILLWELL. Ssshh ! (*He gives John a furious look and motions Father Baird to keep him quiet.*)

FATHER BAIRD. Jack ! Don't you realize you're only harming her ?

JOHN (*confusedly repentant—in a low voice*). I'm sorry. I try not to, but——— I know it's crazy, but I can't help being afraid———

LOVING. That my prophecy is coming true—her end in my story.

JOHN (*with anguished appeal*). No ! Elsa ! Don't believe that !

(*Elsa moans.*)

FATHER BAIRD. You see ! You've disturbed her again !

> (*Stillwell gets up and after exchanging a whispered word with the Nurse, who nods and takes his place by the bedside, comes quickly around the end of the bed to John.*)

STILLWELL. What the devil is the matter with you ? I thought you promised me if I let you stay in here you'd keep quiet.

JOHN (*dazedly now—suddenly overcome by a wave of drowsiness he tries in vain to fight back*). I won't again. (*His head nods.*)

STILLWELL (*gives him a searching look—to Father Baird*). We've got to get him out of here.

JOHN (*rousing himself—desperately fighting back his drowsiness*). I won't sleep ! God, how can I sleep when—— !

STILLWELL (*taking one arm and signalling Father Baird to take the other—sharply but in a voice just above a whisper*). Loving, come into your study. I want to talk with you about your wife's condition.

JOHN (*terrified*). Why ? What do you mean ? She isn't—— ?

STILLWELL (*hastily, in a forced tone of reassurance*). No, no, no ! What put that nonsense in your head ? (*He flashes a signal to the priest and they both lift John to his feet.*) Come along, that's a good fellow.

> (*They lead John to the door to the study at right. Loving follows them silently, moving backward, his eyes fixed with sinister gloating intentness on Elsa's face. Father Baird opens the door and they pass through, Loving slipping after them. Father Baird closes the door. They lead John to the chaise-longue at right, front, of study, passing in front of the table. Loving keeps pace with them, passing to rear of table.*)

JOHN (*starts to resist feebly*). Let me go ! I mustn't leave her ! I'm afraid !

> (*They get him seated on the chaise-longue, Loving taking up a position directly behind him on the other side of the chaise-longue.*)

I feel there's something——

LOVING (*with a gloating mockery*). A demon who laughs, hiding behind the end of my story !

(He gives a sinister laugh. Father Baird and even Stillwell, in spite of himself, are appalled by this laughter.)

JOHN *(starts to his feet—in anguish)*. No !

FATHER BAIRD. Jack !

STILLWELL *(recovering, angry at himself and furious with John—seizes him by the arm and forces him down on the chaise-longue again)*. Stop your damned nonsense ! Get a grip on yourself ! I've warned you you'd go to pieces like this if you kept on refusing to rest or take nourishment. But that's got to stop, do you hear me ? You've got to get some sleep !

FATHER BAIRD. Yes, Jack. You must !

STILLWELL. You've been a disturbing factor from the first and I've been a fool to stand—— But I've had enough ! You'll stay out of her room——

JOHN. No !

STILLWELL. Don't you want her to get well ? By God, from the way you've been acting——

JOHN *(wildly)*. For God's sake, don't say that !

STILLWELL. Can't you see you're no help to her in this condition ? While if you'll sleep for a while——

JOHN. No ! *(Imploringly.)* She's much better, isn't she ? For God's sake, tell me you know she isn't going to—— Tell me that and I'll do anything you ask !

LOVING. And don't lie, please ! I want the truth !

STILLWELL *(forcing an easy tone)*. What's all this talk ? She's resting quietly. There's no question of——

93

(*Then quickly.*) And now I've satisfied you on that, lie down as you promised.

> (*John stares at him uncertainly for a moment—then obediently lies down.*)

Close your eyes now.

> (*John closes his eyes. Loving stands by his head, staring down at his face. John almost immediately drops off into a drugged half-sleep, his breathing becomes heavy and exhausted. Stillwell nods to Father Baird with satisfaction— then moves quietly to the other side of the room, by the door to Elsa's bedroom, beckoning Father Baird to follow him.*)

> (*He speaks to him in a low voice.*)

We'll have to keep an eye on him. He's headed straight for a complete collapse. But I think he'll sleep now, for a while, anyway.

> (*He opens the door to the bedroom, looks in and catches the eye of the Nurse, who is still sitting in the chair by the head of the bed, watching Elsa. The Nurse shakes her head, answering his question. He softly closes the door again.*)

FATHER BAIRD. No change, Doctor ?

STILLWELL. No. But I'm not giving up hope ! She still has a fighting chance ! (*Then in a tone of exasperated dejection.*) If she'd only fight !

FATHER BAIRD (*nods with sad understanding*). Yes. That's it.

STILLWELL. Damn it, she seems to want to die.

(*Then angrily.*) And, by God, in spite of his apparent grief I've suspected at times that underneath he wants——

LOVING (*his eyes fixed on John's face, speaks in a cold, implacable tone*). She is going to die.

JOHN (*starts half-awake—mutters*). No ! Elsa ! Forgive ! (*He sinks into drugged sleep again.*)

STILLWELL. You see. He keeps insisting to him-self——

FATHER BAIRD (*defensively*). That's a horrible charge for you to make, Doctor. Why, anyone can see the poor boy is crazed with fear and grief.

STILLWELL (*a bit ashamed*). Sorry. But there have been times when I've had the strongest sense of—well, as he said, Something—— (*Then curtly, feeling this makes him appear silly.*) Afraid I've allowed this case to get on my nerves. Don't usually go in for psychic nonsense.

FATHER BAIRD. Your feeling isn't nonsense, Doctor.

STILLWELL. She won't forgive him. That's her trouble as well as his. (*He sighs, giving way for a moment to his own physical weariness.*) A strange case. Too many undercurrents. The pneumonia has been more a means than a cause. (*With a trace of condescension.*) More in your line. A little casting out of devils would have been of benefit—might still be.

FATHER BAIRD. Might still be. Yes.

STILLWELL (*exasperatedly*). Damn it, I've seen many worse cases where the patient pulled through. If I could only get her will to live functioning again ! If she'd forgive him and get that off her mind, I know she'd fight. (*He abruptly gets to his feet—curtly.*) Well, talk won't help her, that's sure. I'll get back.

*(He goes into the bedroom and closes the door silently
behind him. Father Baird remains for a
moment staring sadly at the floor. In the bedroom, Stillwell goes to the bedside. The Nurse
gets up and he speaks to her in a whisper,
hears what she has to report, gives her some
quick instructions. She goes to the bathroom.
He sits in the chair by the bed and feels Elsa's
pulse. The Nurse comes back and hands him
a hypodermic needle. He administers this
in Elsa's arm. She moans and her body
twitches for a second. He sits, watching her
face worriedly, his fingers on her wrist. In
the study, Father Baird starts to pace back
and forth, frowning, his face tense, feeling
desperately that he is facing inevitable tragedy,
that he must do something to thwart it at once.
He stops at the foot of the chaise-longue and
stares down at the sleeping John. Then he
prays.)*

FATHER BAIRD. Dear Jesus, grant me the grace to
bring Jack back to Thee. Make him see that Thou,
alone, hast the words of Eternal Life, the power still to
save——

LOVING *(his eyes fixed on John's face in the same stare
—speaks as if in answer to Father Baird's prayer)*. Nothing can save her.

JOHN *(shuddering in his sleep)*. No !

LOVING. Her end in your story is coming true. It
was a cunning method of murder !

FATHER BAIRD *(horrified)*. Jack !

JOHN (*with a tortured cry that starts him awake*). No ! It's a lie ! (*He stares around him at the air, as if he were trying to see some presence he feels there.*) Liar ! Murderer ! (*Suddenly he seems to see Father Baird for the first time—with a cry of appeal—brokenly.*) Uncle ! For God's sake, help me ! I—I feel I'm going mad !

FATHER BAIRD (*eagerly*). If you would only let me help you, Jack ! If you would only be honest with yourself and admit the truth in your own soul now, for Elsa's sake—while there is still time.

JOHN (*frightenedly*). Still time ? What do you mean ? Is she—worse ?

FATHER BAIRD. No. You've only been sleeping a few minutes. There has been no change.

JOHN. Then why did you say——— ?

FATHER BAIRD. Because I have decided you must be told the truth now, the truth you already know in your heart.

JOHN. What—truth ?

FATHER BAIRD. It is the crisis. Human science has done all it can to save her. Her life is in the hands of God now.

LOVING. There is no God !

FATHER BAIRD (*sternly*). Do you dare say that—now !

JOHN (*frightenedly*). No—I—I don't know what I'm saying——— It isn't I———

FATHER BAIRD (*recovering himself—quietly*). No. I know you couldn't blaspheme at such a time—not your true self.

LOVING (*angrily*). It is my true self—my only self ! And I see through your stupid trick—to use the fear of death to——

FATHER BAIRD. It's the hatred you once gave your soul to which speaks, not you ! (*Pleadingly.*) I implore you to cast that evil from your soul ! If you would only pray !

LOVING (*fiercely*). No !

JOHN (*stammers torturedly*). I—I don't know—— I can't think !

FATHER BAIRD (*intensely*). Pray with me, Jack. (*He sinks to his knees.*) Pray that Elsa's life may be spared to you ! It is only God Who can open her heart to forgiveness and give her back the will to live ! Pray for His forgiveness, and He will have compassion on you ! Pray to Him Who is Love. Who is Infinite Tenderness and Pity !

JOHN (*half-slipping to his knees—longingly*). Who is Love ! If I could only believe again !

FATHER BAIRD. Pray for your lost faith and it will be given you !

LOVING (*sneeringly*). You forget I once prayed to your God and His answer was hatred and death—and a mocking laughter !

JOHN (*starts up from his half-kneeling position, under the influence of this memory*). Yes, I prayed then. No. It's no good, Uncle. I can't believe. (*Then suddenly —with eagerness.*) Let Him prove to me His Love exists ! Then I will believe in Him again !

FATHER BAIRD. You may not bargain with your

God, Jack. (*He gets wearily to his feet, his shoulders bowed, looking tragically old and beaten—then with a last appeal.*) But I beseech you still ! I warn you !— before it's too late !—look into your soul and force yourself to admit the truth you find there—the truth you have yourself revealed in your story where the man, who is you, goes to the church and, at the foot of the Cross, is granted the grace of faith again !

LOVING. In a moment of stupid madness ! But remember that is not the end !

FATHER BAIRD (*ignoring this*). There is a fate in that story, Jack—the fate of the will of God made manifest to you through the secret longing of your own heart for faith ! Take care ! It has come true so far, and I am afraid if you persist in your mad denial of Him and your own soul, you will have willed for yourself the accursed end of that man—and for Elsa, death !

JOHN (*terrified*). Stop ! Stop talking damned nonsense ! (*Distractedly.*) Leave me alone ! I'm sick of your damned croaking ! You're lying ! Stillwell said there was no danger ! She's asleep ! She's getting better ! (*Then terrified again.*) What made you say, a fate in my story—the will of God ? Good God, that's —that's nonsense ! I—— (*He starts for the bedroom door.*) I'm going back to her. There's Something——

FATHER BAIRD (*tries to hold him back*). You can't go there now, Jack.

JOHN (*pushing him roughly away*). Leave me alone !

(*He opens the bedroom door and lurches in. Loving has come around behind the table and slips in after him. Father Baird, recovering from the*

99

push which has sent him back against the table, front, comes quickly to the doorway.)
(As John comes in, Stillwell turns from where he sits beside the bedside, a look of intense anger and exasperation on his face. John, as soon as he enters, falls under the atmosphere of the sick-room, his wildness drops from him and he looks at Stillwell with pleading eyes.)

STILLWELL *(giving up getting him out again as hopeless, makes a gesture for him to be silent)*.   Ssshh !

(The Nurse looks at John with shocked rebuke. Stillwell motions John to sit down. He does so meekly, sinking into the chair at right, centre. Loving stands behind the chair. Father Baird, after a look into the room to see if his help is needed, exchanges a helpless glance with Stillwell, and then, turning back into the study but leaving the communicating door ajar, goes back as far as the table. There, after a moment's pause, he bows his head and begins praying silently to himself. In the bedroom, Stillwell turns back to his patient. There is a pause of silent immobility in the room. John's eyes are fixed on Elsa's face with a growing terror. Loving stares over his head with cold, still eyes.)

JOHN *(in a low, tense voice—as if he were thinking aloud)*.   A fate in my story—the will of God !   Something——   *(He shudders.)*

LOVING *(in the same low tone, but with a cold, driving intensity)*.   She will soon be dead.

JOHN.   No !

LOVING. What will you do then ? Love will be lost to you for ever. You will be alone again. There will remain only the anguish of endless memories, endless regrets—a torturing remorse for murdered happiness !

JOHN. I know ! For God's sake, don't make me think——

LOVING (*coldly remorseless—sneeringly*). Do you think you can choose your stupid end in your story now, when you have to live it ?—on to Hercules ? But if you love her, how can you desire to go on—with all that was Elsa rotting in her grave behind you !

JOHN (*torturedly*). No ! I can't ! I'll kill myself !

ELSA (*suddenly moans frightenedly*). No, John ! No !

LOVING (*triumphantly*). Ah ! At last you accept the true end ! At last you see the empty posing of your old ideal about man's duty to go on for Life's sake, your meaningless gesture of braving fate—a childish nose-thumbing at Nothingness at which Something laughs with a weary scorn ! (*He gives a low, scornful laugh.*) Shorn of your boastful words, all it means is to go on like an animal in dumb obedience to the law of the blind stupidity of life that it must live at all costs ! But where will you go—except to death ? And why should you wait for an end you know when it is in your power to grasp that end—now !

ELSA (*again moans frightenedly*). No, John—no !—please, John !

LOVING. Surely you cannot be afraid of death. Death is not the dying. Dying is life, its last revenge upon itself. But death is what the dead know, the warm, dark womb of Nothingness—the Dream in which you and Elsa may sleep as one for ever, beyond fear of separation !

JOHN (*longingly*). Elsa and I—for ever beyond fear !

LOVING. Dust within dust to sleep !

JOHN (*mechanically*). Dust within dust. (*Then frightenedly questioning.*) Dust ? (*A shudder runs over him and he starts as if awakening from sleep.*) Fool ! Can the dust love the dust ? No ! (*Desperately.*) Oh God, have pity ! Show me the way !

LOVING (*furiously—as if he felt himself temporarily beaten*). Coward !

JOHN. If I could only pray ! If I could only believe again !

LOVING. You cannot !

JOHN. A fate in my story, Uncle said—the will of God !—I went to the church—a fate in the church—— (*He suddenly gets to his feet as if impelled by some force outside him. He stares before him with obsessed eyes.*) Where I used to believe, where I used to pray !

LOVING. You insane fool ! I tell you that's ended !

JOHN. If I could see the Cross again——

LOVING (*with a shudder*). No ! I don't want to see ! I remember too well !—when Father and Mother—— !

JOHN. Why are you so afraid of Him, if——

LOVING (*shaken—then with fierce defiance*). Afraid ? I who once cursed Him, who would again if—— (*Then hurriedly catching himself.*) But what superstitious nonsense you make me remember. He doesn't exist !

JOHN (*takes a step toward the door*). I am going !

LOVING (*tries to bar his path*). No!

JOHN (*without touching him, makes a motion of pushing him aside*). I am going.

> (*He goes through the door to the study, moving like one in a trance, his eyes fixed straight before him. Loving continues to try to bar his path, always without touching him. Father Baird looks up as they pass the table.*)

LOVING (*in impotent rage*). No! You coward!

> (*John goes out the door in rear of study and Loving is forced out before him.*)

FATHER BAIRD (*starting after him*). Jack!

> (*But he turns back in alarm as, in the bedroom, Elsa suddenly comes out of the half-coma she is in with a cry of terror and, in spite of Stillwell, springs up to a half-sitting position in bed, her staring eyes on the doorway to the study.*)

ELSA. John! (*Then to Stillwell.*) Oh, please! Look after him! He might—— John! Come back! I'll forgive!

STILLWELL (*soothingly*). There, don't be frightened. He's only gone to lie down for a while. He's very tired.

> (*Father Baird has come in from the study and is approaching the bed. Stillwell, with a significant look, calls on him for confirmation.*)

Isn't that right, Father?

FATHER BAIRD. Yes, Elsa.

ELSA (*relieved*). Oh! (*She smiles faintly.*) Poor John. I'm so sorry. Tell him he mustn't worry. I understand now. I love—I forgive.

(*She sinks back and closes her eyes. Stillwell reaches for her wrist in alarm, but as he feels her pulse his expression changes to one of excited surprise.*)

FATHER BAIRD (*misreading his look—in a frightened whisper*). Merciful God ! She isn't—— ?

STILLWELL. No. She's asleep. (*Then with suppressed excitement.*) That's done it ! She'll want to live now !

FATHER BAIRD. God be praised !

(*Stillwell, his air curtly professional, again turns and whispers some orders to the Nurse.*)

CURTAIN

SCENE TWO

SCENE. *A section of the interior of an old church. A side wall runs diagonally back from left, front, two-thirds of the width of the stage, where it meets an end wall that extends back from right, front. The walls are old grey stone. In the middle of the side wall is a great cross, its base about five feet from the floor, with a life-size figure of Christ, an exceptionally fine piece of wood carving. In the middle of the end wall is an arched doorway. On either side of this door, but high up in the wall, their bases above the level of the top of the doorway, are two narrow, stained-glass windows.*

It is a few minutes after the close of the preceding scene. The church is dim and empty, and still. The only light is the reflection of the dawn, which, stained by the colour in the windows, falls on the wall on and around the Cross.

The outer doors beyond the arched doorway are suddenly pushed open with a crash and John and Loving appear in the doorway. Loving comes first, retreating backward before John whom he desperately, but always without touching him, endeavours to keep from entering the church. But John is the stronger now and, the same look of obsessed resolution in his eyes, he forces Loving back.

LOVING (*as they enter—desperately, as if he were becoming exhausted by the struggle*). You fool ! There is nothing here but hatred !

JOHN. No ! There was love ! (*His eyes fasten themselves on the Cross and he gives a cry of hope.*) The Cross !

LOVING. The symbol of hate and derision !

JOHN. No ! Of love !

> (*Loving is forced back until the back of his head is against the foot of the Cross. John throws himself on his knees before it and raises his hands up to the figure of Christ in supplication.*)

Mercy ! Forgive !

LOVING (*raging*). Fool ! Grovel on your knees ! It is useless ! To pray, one must believe !

JOHN. I have come back to Thee !

LOVING. Words ! There is nothing !

JOHN. Let me believe in Thy love again !

LOVING.   You cannot believe !

JOHN (*imploringly*).   O God of Love, hear my prayer !

LOVING.   There is no God !   There is only death !

JOHN (*more weakly now*).   Have pity on me !   Let Elsa live !

LOVING.   There is no pity !   There is only scorn !

JOHN.   Hear me while there is still time ! (*He waits, staring at the Cross with anguished eyes, his arms outstretched.   There is a pause of silence.*)

LOVING (*with triumphant mockery*).   Silence !   But behind it I hear mocking laughter !

JOHN (*agonized*).   No ! (*He gives way, his head bowed, and sobs heartbrokenly—then stops suddenly, and looking up at the Cross again, speaks sobbingly in a strange humble tone of broken reproach.*)   O Son of Man, I am Thou and Thou art I !   Why hast Thou forsaken me ? O Brother Who lived and loved and suffered and died with us, Who knoweth the tortured hearts of men, canst Thou not forgive—now—when I surrender all to Thee—when I have forgiven Thee—the love that Thou once took from me !

LOVING (*with a cry of hatred*).   No !   Liar !   I will never forgive !

JOHN (*his eyes fixed on the face of the Crucified suddenly lighting up as if he now saw there the answer to his prayer —in a voice trembling with awakening hope and joy*).   Ah ! Thou hast heard me at last !   Thou hast not forsaken me !   Thou hast always loved me !   I am forgiven ! I can forgive myself—through Thee !   I can believe !

LOVING (*stumbles weakly from beneath the Cross*). No !
I deny ! (*He turns to face the Cross with a last defiance.*)
I defy Thee ! Thou canst not conquer me ! I hate
Thee ! I curse Thee !

JOHN. No ! I bless ! I love !

LOVING (*as if this were a mortal blow, seems to sag and
collapse—with a choking cry*). No !

JOHN (*with a laugh that is half sob*). Yes ! I see now !
At last I see ! I have always loved ! O Lord of Love,
forgive Thy poor blind fool !

LOVING. No ! (*His legs crumple under him, he slumps
to his knees beside John, as if some invisible force crushed him
down.*)

JOHN (*his voice rising exultantly, his eyes on the face of
the Crucified*). Thou art the Way—the Truth—the
Resurrection and the Life, and he that believeth in Thy
Love, his love shall never die !

LOVING (*faintly, at last surrendering, addressing the
Cross not without a final touch of pride in his humility*).
Thou hast conquered, Lord. Thou art—the End.
Forgive—the damned soul—of John Loving !

> (*He slumps forward to the floor and rolls over on his
> back, dead, his head beneath the foot of the
> Cross, his arms outflung so that his body forms
> another cross. John rises from his knees and
> stands with arms stretched up and out, so that
> he, too, is like a cross. While this is happening
> the light of the dawn on the stained-glass
> windows swiftly rises to a brilliant intensity of*

crimson and green and gold, as if the sun had risen. The grey walls of the church, particularly the wall where the Cross is, and the face of the Christ shine with this radiance.)

John Loving—he, who had been only John—remains standing with his arms stretched up to the Cross, an expression of mystic exaltation on his face. The corpse of Loving lies at the foot of the Cross, like a cured cripple's testimonial offering in a shrine.

(Father Baird comes in hurriedly through the arched doorway. He stops on seeing John Loving, then comes quietly up beside him and stares searchingly into his face. At what he sees there he bows his head and his lips move in grateful prayer. John Loving is oblivious to his presence.)

FATHER BAIRD (*finally taps him gently on the shoulder*). Jack.

JOHN LOVING (*still in his ecstatic mystic vision—strangely*). I am John Loving.

FATHER BAIRD (*stares at him—gently*). It's all right now, Jack. Elsa will live.

JOHN LOVING (*exaltedly*). I know! Love lives forever! Death is dead! Ssshh! Listen! Do you hear?

FATHER BAIRD. Hear what, Jack?

JOHN LOVING. Life laughs with God's love again! Life laughs with love!

CURTAIN

Europe in a Motorhome

A Mid-Life Gap Year
Around Southern Europe

H D Jackson

TRAFFORD
PUBLISHING

USA • Canada • UK • Ireland

Note for Librarians: A cataloguing record for this book is available from Library and Archives Canada at www.collectionscanada.ca/amicus/index-e.html
ISBN 1-4120-8141-6

Printed on paper with minimum 30% recycled fibre.
Trafford's print shop runs on "green energy" from solar, wind and other environmentally-friendly power sources.

TRAFFORD
PUBLISHING™
Offices in Canada, USA, Ireland and UK

Book sales for North America and international:
Trafford Publishing, 6E–2333 Government St.,
Victoria, BC V8T 4P4 CANADA
phone 250 383 6864 (toll-free 1 888 232 4444)
fax 250 383 6804; email to orders@trafford.com
Book sales in Europe:
Trafford Publishing (UK) Limited, 9 Park End Street, 2nd Floor
Oxford, UK OX1 1HH UNITED KINGDOM
phone 44 (0)1865 722 113 (local rate 0845 230 9601)
facsimile 44 (0)1865 722 868; info.uk@trafford.com
Order online at:
trafford.com/05-3138

10 9 8 7 6 5 4